Handmaid

Handmaid

The Power of Names in Theology and Society

CAROLINE N. MBONU

WIPF & STOCK · Eugene, Oregon

HANDMAID
The Power of Names in Theology and Society

Copyright © 2010 Caroline N. Mbonu. All rights reserved. Except for brief quotations in critical publications or reviews, no part of this book may be reproduced in any manner without prior written permission from the publisher. Write: Permissions, Wipf and Stock Publishers, 199 W. 8th Ave., Suite 3, Eugene, OR 97401.

Wipf & Stock
An Imprint of Wipf and Stock Publishers
199 W. 8th Ave., Suite 3
Eugene, OR 97401
www.wipfandstock.com

ISBN 13: 978-1-60899-761-9

Manufactured in the U.S.A.

All scripture quotations, unless otherwise indicated, are taken from the Holy Bible, New International Version®, NIV®. Copyright ©1973, 1978, 1984 by Biblica, Inc.™ Used by permission of Zondervan. All rights reserved worldwide.

I dedicate this work
to the Ever Green Memory
of Nwada Nwaiwu and Onyegorom Nwaoghu, my parents
Nwaōghu Nwanguma Nwanyimenini and Mbonu Okere Nwankwoala,
my grandparents
and
Sister Catherine Archibong, HHCJ

Contents

Preface ix
Acknowledgments xi
Introduction xiii

1 **HANDMAID: SITUATING THE WORD** 1
- Introduction
- The Bible and African Perspective
- The Handmaid: Ecclesial Appropriation
- The Handmaid: A Contemporary Understanding
- The Handmaid: an African Adaptation

2 **HANDMAID: THE *DOULĒ* AND ISRAEL'S *DOULAS* FIGURES** 17
- Introduction

A Hebraic Understanding of the Terms `ebed, doulē paidiskē
- Word Study: *Doul*-stem
- *Doul*-stem Word in the Hebrew Tradition
- *Doul*-stem Word in Ancient Literature
- *Doul*-stem Word in the New Testament
- *Doul*-stem Word in Christian Arts and Literature
- *Doul*-stem Word in Igbo Tradition

Doulas Figures in the Hebrew Bible and in the Septuagint
- *Doulē* Ruth
- *Doulē* Abigail
- *Doulē* Esther
- *Doulē* Judith

3 **THE HANDMAID: MARY OF NAZARETH** 38
- Introduction
- *Doulē* Tradition
- Establishing Identity
- The Text: Luke 1:26–38
- Historical Background

Close Reading of of Luke 1:26–38
- Rhetorical Analysis
- Mary Speaks: First Voice in the Synoptic Gospels
- Mary and Zachariah
- Ideology: Discipleship
- Conclusion

4 THE POWER OF NAMING IN AFRICAN-IGBO CULTURE 64

- Introduction
- The Retelling: The Significance of Stories in African
- Metaphor and Cultural Idioms

Significance of Name
Name and Naming: Deconstruct and Reconstruct
- *Anthills of the Savannah*
- Beatrice Nwanyibuife
- Kimpa Vita (c. 1682—1706), Beatrice of the Congo
- Beatrice Nwanyibuife and Amaechina
- Reflection on Contemporary Female Names
- Nwanyikwa
- Women, the Jewish Experience: Bread Givers
- Ejinwanyiemenini
- Women in Traditional Igbo Social Life
- *Ogu Umunwanyi*, Women's War, 1929–1931
- Renaming the Girl-Child
- Retelling: The Story

The *Doulē* Metaphor Revisited
- Conclusion

5 THE *DOULĒ*: BIBLICAL AND CONTEMPORARY 108

- Introduction

Revisiting Biblical Reflections: The *Doulē* of Nazareth
The Woman of Shunem (2 Kgs 4:8–37)
Mother Mary Charles Magdalen Walker, RSC and the
    Congregation of the Handmaids of the Holy Child Jesus
A Woman in the Global Village: Reclaiming Identify

Glossary 129
Bibliography 131

Preface

Handmaid: The Power of Names in Theology and Society

THE INTEREST TO WRITE this book emerges from my own experience and scholarship and reflects on the themes of service, leadership, dignity, and agency. For many years, I have studied, reflected, contemplated, and struggled with the idea of the image of Mary in Christianity. The quest for understanding Mary and the way in which she influences women in the faith heightened with my lived experience as a professed member in a religious community of women named after Mary: Handmaids of the Holy Child Jesus. In addition, my training in biblical studies and Christian spirituality has brought maturity to my thoughts and understanding of Mary. Drawing from Luke 1:26-38, the book provides a glimpse of Mary's self-understanding, as *Doulē kyriou*, Greek term for "servant of the LORD." Mary's self-understanding as *doulē kuriou* tends to escape the attention and imagination of exegetes who often cast her in a subordinate position, literally, the handmaid, meaning one who accompanies in a subordinate capacity. Growing up Roman Catholic, the image of Mary communicated to me was that of a woman utterly passive. Although this image has stayed with me, it does not resonate with my experience as a woman, or with that of the women in my life, specifically, my mother and my grandmother. My matriarchal forbearers did not appear passive; they were servants as well as leaders in the home and in the community. Furthermore, I draw from textual and oral literature, particularly of the African-Igbo to show how certain names, like the designation handmaid, can be used to construct women. What I attempt to do in this work is to offer a thought on revalorizing women's agency through a redemptive reading of biblical and cultural name texts. It is my hope that this Lukan passage can become the key that unlocks and makes possible a redreaming of a new image of women in church and in society.

I also hope that *Handmaid: The Power of Names in Theology and Society*, will awaken the curiosity of many in Mary, the quintessential symbol of womanhood in Christianity. This book provides a glimpse of the experience and perspective of the silenced, and those on the margins. Having come from the shadows of patriarchy, Mary emerges with a voice of her own and takes the center stage in the Lukan narrative. Hailing from an insignificant community, where we find the absentees of history, positions the story as a liberative tale—a tale "from below." The voice shines a light on the handmaidens of our world, creating a fissure through which a new possibility can emerge. This book also raises real questions about justice and spirituality that will challenge and inspire the reader. Most importantly, it will shine a light on the experience of women in society and in church life.

Acknowledgments

E*KELE DIRI CHUKWU*. I owe a great deal to more people than I can possible acknowledge here. Many helped to make this book possible. First I express my deepest gratitude to my religious community, the Handmaids of the Holy Child Jesus, Central Eastern Province for the spirituality that supports this project and the opportunity given me to study and to write. I am grateful to the Graduate Theological Union, Berkeley for the financial assistance without which I could not have completed my doctoral program. I am grateful to those who helped me to focus and refine the position from which this book grew, especially Fr. Eduardo Fernandez, S.J., my dissertation director. I thank the other members of my committee for their painstaking supervision: Dr. Judy Siker, Fr. William O'Neill, S.J., and Prof. Jacob Olupona of Harvard University whose research on gender and African religious traditions greatly enriched my perspectives. I am grateful to Fr. Kenan B. Osborne, OFM, Prof. Judith Berling, and Fr. John Endres, S.J. for their support of my scholarship. I am equally thankful to Father Lawrence Frizzell of the Department of Jewish-Christian Studies, Seton Hall University, New Jersey, who read the initial manuscript and offered invaluable suggestions. My spiritual director, Father George Murphy, SJ, helped me to keep soul and body together in Berkeley! I thank my colleagues at the Graduate Theological Union, Berkeley, particularly, Sister Carolyn Roeber, O.P., Patricia Vanni, Sister Margaret Gorman, SND, Sister Margaret Aringo, FSJ, Pius Ojara, S.J., Fathers. B. Kwame Assenyoh, SVD, Victor Adangba, S.J., Ehi Omoragbon, S.J., Deogratis Rwezaura, S.J., and specially Emmanuel Foro, S.J. who played the "devil's advocate" in my redemptive reading of the *Doulē* in Luke 1:26-38. I am grateful to those who read my manuscript at various stages of its development including Lissa Dirrim, Fr. Chukwuma Okoye, C.ss.P., Janie Wilson, Dr. Christopher Brooks, Dr. Fabian Udoh, Dr. John Whaley, and Fr. Okechukwu Camilius Njoku, who helped me with the Etche-Igbo dialet.

I am grateful for friendship of my community(HHCJ) Sisters, especially, Sisters Rose Ereba, Bernedette Ezeyi, Mary Rita Abang, Anastasia Njoku, Stella Maris Ihejieto, Ngozi Uti, Immaculata Chukwuyere, Helen Umeh, Caroline Onyeoziri, Stella Chibuoke, Bibiana Okoro, Rosemary Arrah, and Romanna Uzodinmma. I specially thank the many friends who provided spiritual, moral, and financial support, The Franciscan Handmaids of Mary, and Sisters Loretta Theresa Richards, FHM, Maria Goretti Mannix, FHM and Gertrude Ihenacho, FHM in particular. I thank my "mother," Mrs. Hotenzia Pogany for many happy memories. Along with her I am grateful to Magdaline Ohia, Dr. Regina Bioclair, Dr. Dorothy Duff Brown, Amadiebube and Claudia Mbama, Dr. Etim and Theresa Udowana, Silas and Ngozi Agbim, Becky and Jeff Davis, Fr. August Thompson, The Selesians of Don Bosco, Berkeley, Most Rev. A. O. Makozi, Msgr. Theophilus Okere, Fr. Joseph Kabari, Msgr. Cyprian Onwuli, Msgr. John K. Wangbu, Fr. Wencelasus Madu, CMF, Fr. Donatus Ukulor, Fr. Paulinus Odozor, Fr. Brendan Mbagwu. I am grateful to Mrs. Kaffy Balineaux Belvin and Fr Maurice Nut, C.Ss.R. for their assistance in proofreading the text. To my wonderful siblings, Nwaobira, Nnenne, Nwaobilor, Uwakwe, Onyinyechi, Uwanaghiakwa and Chibuzor, I owe you a deep gratitude for *ahunwanne. Otito diri Chikiokeke.*

Caroline Mbonu, HHCJ,
Richmond, Virginia, 2010

Introduction

THE STIMULUS TO WRITE this book came from two sources. One is the experience of growing up in a society as a female and participating in anything I wanted. At a certain age I was made to understand that I could not take part in some activities, because I was "not a male," meaning that I was "the other." This restriction or rather exclusion left a deep impression on me. It led me to ask the question, why?

The other, perhaps the foundational reason for this project, came from the image of Mary in the Roman Catholic piety and devotion, in my personal experience as an avowed religious of over thirty years. The attention given to this icon of Christianity awakened a profound curiosity in me. My story emerged from wrestling with the name "Handmaid" and seeking out its liberative potential which I understand to include words, actions, or events that unburden, lift up, or promote the humanity of persons, individuals, and collective groups in the face of oppression. I write this book, *Handmaid: The Power of Names in Theology and Society* as a liberative project, as well as a vehicle to further the Good news.

The stance I have taken in writing this book resonates with my embodied experience as a member of a religious community of women named after Mary, The Handmaids of the Holy Child Jesus. This experience made me acutely aware of the structures established and protected by the dominant culture; structures that limit women's full participation in society, as well as church life. These excluding structures seem to have the effect of emptying the Gospel message of its meaning, the Good News.

The Bible, undoubtedly a foundational text in Western civilization, continues to influence the social, cultural, and religious contexts of many societies. Although sacred to only a small percentage of the human race, the Bible exerts enormous influence well beyond the confines of those who subscribe to its meaning. Historically, Scripture has been in the forefront of major changes, from the monastic movement of the early centuries to the recent era of the Second Vatican Council. The cruel and often barbaric history of African enslavement and colonization also had scriptural sanction. Biblical interpretation, however, continued to act as catalysts for societal changes such as antislavery crusaders and general human rights concerns through the centuries. This means that the radicalism of the Gospel message always brings epoch-marking changes. The narrative I relate in this book follows a similar path of bringing positive changes that can enhance the human attempt to flourish together as male and female in society, as well as church life. Excluding any gender or group of persons from full participation in social processes deprives humanity of the full synergy of human potential. I employ the image of Mary of Nazareth as described in Luke 1:26–38 to make my contribution.

This book is an attempt to understand Mary's private voice in her assertion as the *doulē kyriou*, (two Greek words: *doulē*, servant and *kyriou*, LORD), hence, servant of the LORD. In so doing, Mary's private voice becomes a public voice for women, as well as men, in their vocation as servants of each other in the community (Luke 22:27). I capitalize the word LORD, meaning the God of Israel, as emphasis.

The image of Mary, particularly her role as the maidservant of Nazareth continues to dominate the popular perception of this woman whose contribution to humanity has had a continuing historical significance in our world. But that idea of maidservant translated as Handmaid tends to reduce her significance. The idea of Handmaid, translated in formal English as a principle that has an important part in supporting or helping another idea tends to downplay the role of this valiant woman in her cooperating with God's plan of fostering salvation and redemption, communion, and reconciliation. Thus this translation tends to minimize Mary's agency, shutting her out of social processes. As Handmaid, therefore, Mary of Nazareth was never a subject but always an object, supportive and secondary, thereby trivialized and marginalized. Thus the freight that the name or the designation Handmaid carries, places one so designated in a permanent subordinate position. To investigate the name designation, Handmaid, therefore, becomes a critical step in rethinking women's situation in Africa. In most African societies, a name functions as a place-holder, social location, and a part of belonging. In some sense, a name represents the essential characters or circumstances surrounding individuals at the time of their birth. Thus a pejorative or an inane designation can damage one's psyche, just as a positive or affirmative name can foster personal creativity. Hence, I embark on a critical discussion and a retelling of the story of the Handmaid of Nazareth as the servant of the LORD, *doulē kyriou*, and interpreting certain names given to the girl-child in the African-Igbo society.

Mary's self-understanding as *doulē kyriou* in Luke 1:38, suggests a creative response. The word *doulē* exists in contradistinction to *paidiskē*, which has other associations. While leading biblical women characters call themselves *doulē/doulas*, *paidiskē* is a designation given to female abject servants, handmaidens or slave women. In religious circles, however, *paidiskē* has gained currency as emblematic of the biblical handmaid. My choice for the metaphor speaks of positive retrieval of the potential and human dignity of the *doulē*. Metaphors associate two terms that do not belong together. In this Lukan passage, an ordinary Jewish maiden from an insignificant village, Nazareth, is set against an extraordinary background. The tension between these two settings provokes an insight that reveals new depths in familiar material.

Evidence in the Lukan passage (1:26–38), lends support to the new materials that I draw from to weave my narrative. Data from the narrative does not seem to represent this Nazarene Handmaid in the sense of *paidiskē*. Rather, Mary presents herself as a *doulē kyriou* in the same sense that Moses was *doulos theou* (God), Servant of God. Thus Mary's self-understanding is captured in the name she takes for herself, *doulē kyriou*, the servant of the LORD. Such understanding did not suggest one who accompanied in a subordinate manner, which the English translation Handmaid evokes. In this regard, the designation *doulē* becomes an interpretative tool, which enables the weaving of this story; hence the title of my book, *Handmaid: The Power of Name in Theology and Society*.

Since the history and construction of identity is marked and shaped by plural narratives, it become imperative to retrieve Mary's self-understanding in the Lukan story. Storytelling as a form of remembrance unmasks critically and creatively opens people's eyes, so that by remembering, they can see, understand and believe. The Benin theologian, Valentin Dedji, echoes other African scholars to maintain that, "Story-telling, in one form or another, is part of all traditions, cultures and civilizations. Africa is specifically a place of story-telling. Although it takes time for true stories to be told, stories that reveal the sacredness of life, that point to events that have hurt and healed, given life and death, are not easy stories to tell".[1] Retrieval and a reinterpretation of this Lukan *doulē* can enable it to become a liberative and redemptive story, not only for women but for men as well.

My interest in writing this book represents the human desire to live, share, and enjoy life with others, which necessitates reinterpreting, retooling, or restructuring the instruments of exclusion and reshaping them into instruments that can further liberative causes. The practical place to begin is to engage the very instrument of exclusion, in this case, construction of identity, which the name and the naming process strongly support. Investigating Scripture and searching for clues to the self-understanding of Mary as *doulē kyriou* becomes very significant.

I tell this story drawing first from my experience and out of my scholarly disciplines, New Testament, Contemporary African Christian Theology, Christian Spirituality, and my context as a Roman Catholic religious from the community of the Handmaids of the Holy Child Jesus as well as an African of Igbo ethnic origin. Naturally, my continental African background provides the language and pattern of thought with which I can tell the story of Mary, the young Jewish maiden from an insignificant Galilean village, Nazareth. The significance of what God can accomplish in an obscure setting can resonate with many in such insignificant places, who strive to live a Christian life as revealed by Jesus of Nazareth.

Drawing from the Scriptures as well as the works of African women theologians, I began to explore a redemptive interpretation of the image of Mary. Insights derived from my investigation and personal experiences have enabled me to weave a cloth that is representative of women's fuller humanity. I call this cloth *Akwete*. *Akwete* is a rich woven cloth indigenous to Igbo culture. The intense, differentiated, beautiful, and sturdy, qualities of the tapestry function metaphorically in representing idioms that foster fullness of life. But most especially, the *Akwete* metaphor symbolizes images of positive self-identification for women. It is my hope that the insights I bring to this story will contribute in re-introducing women as representatives and agents of God's saving action in the community of humankind.

Presented in five chapters, the story evolves into a pair of complements producing a chalice-like shaped design. Chapter one comple-

---

1. Dedji, *Reconstruction & Renewal*, 82.

ments chapter five. Both chapters represent time—the past, present and future history. In a similar manner, chapter two complements chapter four. The two chapters speak to and interrogate each other, investigating the meaning of the designation, *doulē* from biblical sources and female names in Igbo culture. The heart of the story, resides in chapter three: a redemptive reading of Handmaid in the sense of *doulē*. The chalice-like structure of this project suggests the efficacy of this undertaking, a Eucharistic motif. While Baptism introduces us into the faith community, the Eucharist sustains and nourishes the faithful. The Eucharistic theme fits into a redemptive image, which the metaphor of the *doulē* symbolizes.

In a world that is becoming increasingly interconnected, I situate African society, in chapter one, within a wider Judeo-Christian context to establish the validity of this narrative. For this work to be a truly liberative project, good news, that is glad tidings (Isa 61:1–2); a denunciation of the pervasive oppressive structure that limits women's participation in social processes must precede the annunciation of the good news. Otherwise, the message will merely buttress the sinful status quo. Thus in this chapter, I critique certain ecclesial and cultural appropriations of the designation "Handmaid."

In chapter two I explore the metaphorical Hebraic understanding of Handmaid in the sense of *doulē*. Although the Greek usage in the Septuagint (LXX) might suggest Hellenistic usage of the word and the social context of the Greek world, the metaphorical usage has to be understood in terms of its usage in the Hebrew Bible. This denotation of the *doul*-stem word, agrees with the characteristics of the Lukan *doulē*. I seek insights from four Israelite biblical characters, Ruth, Abigail, Esther, and Judith to show how the Lukan *doulē* represents a type of these savior figures.

In chapter three I develop and confirm the thesis of my book. The chapter investigates the Lukan handmaid. It shows to whom Mary belongs and to what she is committed. Thus, I occupy myself with an exegetical and interpretative reweaving of the pericope, Luke 1:26–38. My analysis establishes the identity of Mary, the Jewish teenager, who designates herself the handmaid of the LORD. It further explores the issue of voice. Mary's first voice recorded in the Synoptics. In addition, I examine the contrast between Mary and Zachariah. I also explain the concept of discipleship as service in leadership, the quintessential quality of the *doulē kyriou*.

Drawing from textual and oral history, I discuss the name and naming as critical tools for the construction of "female" identity in chapter four. The discussion fits into the freight that the name designation "Handmaid" carries. I retell, in a liberative manner, women's stories from two novels, one African and one Jewish: Chinua Achebe's *Anthills of the Savannah* and Anzia Yezierska, *Bread Givers*. Two African names Nwanwanyikwa (*Nwa-nwa-nyi-kwa*), "a female child again!" and *Ejinwanwanyiemenini?* (*Eji-nwa-nwa-nyi-em-ni-ni?*), "what can one do with a female child?" In effect, this chapter is about deconstructing and reconstructing women's identity through name and naming.

In the fifth and concluding chapter, I concern myself with the appropriation and adaptation of the qualities of the *doulē kyriou* for the contemporary woman. To this end, I employ biblical narrative of the woman of Shunem, and Mother Mary Charles Magdalen Walker (RSC) and the religious community she founded, Handmaids of the Holy Child Jesus as the warp and woof for weaving a new cloth, one more representative of women as *doulas*, in society and church life. In the end, the goal of appropriation is connected with enabling people to discover the kingdom "among you" (Luke 17: 21).

It my hope that this book would serve as a valuable textbook for courses in gender studies, biblical studies, and women's spirituality and will be of special interest to others, such as theologians, some of whom are researching feminist/womanist issues. *Handmaid* would also be of interest to formators in religious communities or seminaries, as well as those who will be educating young people in high school for college. The story I have retold in these pages can also become an added asset for religious communities in the active renewal of their charisms. The *Dogmatic Constitution on Divine revelation, Dei Verbum*, makes clear that Scripture is the soul of theology and that the study of Scripture is never finished, because each age must newly seek to understand the sacred books.[2] My retelling of the story of Mary of Nazareth represents one such attempt to newly understand the sacred text and enrich the theological reflection of this icon of Christianity, at the same time proposing this new understanding as a liberative tool for every Christian.

---

2. Béchard, ed. "*Scripture Documents*," 244.

Biblical references and translation utilized in this book represent those from the Bible texts: *The Catholic Study Bible, The New American Bible*, Second edition, eds. Donald Senior and John J. Collins (Oxford: Oxford University Press, 2006), *The New Oxford Annotated Bible New Revised Standard Version with the Apocrypha. Third edition.* Oxford: Oxford University Press, 2001, *Nestle-Aland Greek-English New Testament, English Revised Edition*, 2nd Printing (Deutsche Bibelgesellschaft, 1998), *Bible Nso: Testament Ochie na Testament Ohuru.* Suffolk, Great Britain: Richard Clay, 1996, and *Baibul Nso Nhazi Katolik.* Onitsha, Nigeria: Africana-Fep Publishers, 2000. My use of inclusive language shows in the interchanging of gender pronouns. It is my hope that this book, which continues to shape my sense of service, would represent a voice of a human community striving to flourish together.

1

Handmaid: Situating the Word

Introduction

SCRIPTURE HAS BEEN IN the forefront of major changes from the monastic movement of the early centuries to the recent era of the Second Vatican Council.[1] Indeed, during the period of the Renaissance, which witnessed renewed interest in the classical culture of the ancient world, Scriptural revival featured prominently.[2] This means that the radicalism of the Gospel message always brings epoch-marking changes. Biblical interpretations have acted as catalysts for societal changes for centuries, and biblical principles have informed humans of the infinite worth of the individual and the call to fight against evil.[3]

For the people of the biblical tradition, Scripture provides the language we need to discern and describe evil. Therefore, any contemporary study that would advance the cause of humanity in a globalized ambience cannot ignore the influence of Scripture.

Employing biblical texts to advance the cause of women allows me to highlight the critical roles women play in redemption history. Luke makes explicit this claim by placing a woman, Mary of Nazareth, at the center of the Incarnation narrative (Luke 1:26–38). If the good news, that is, the reign of God, means those on the margins have become part of the larger conversation, then this Lukan narrative clearly accomplishes that purpose. Moreover, by telling this story, the author emphasizes that God's reign will be socially transforming. The English scholar, Sarah Jane

---

1. Béchard, ed. *"Scripture Documents,"* 272.
2. González, *The Story of Christianity, Volume 2*, 10, 185.
3. Tolbert, "Defining the Problem: The Biblical and Feminist Hermeneutics," 120.

Boss posits that Christians down through the centuries have variously conceptualized Mary of Nazareth at some time as the wielder of Christ's imperial authority, and at other times as the submissive maiden of Nazareth.[4] The wide range of thought grounded in the different cultures and epochs that appropriate Mary's role makes possible an interpretation of this Nazareth maiden in contemporary African expressions.

The Nigerian New Testament scholar, Justin Ukpong, makes a case for African Bible scholarship. Ukpong contends that Africans must not think that the field of biblical scholarship is closed, leaving us to tread behind the West in desperation. He insists that we use our African perspectives and contextual insights to formulate our own questions. Furthermore, Ukpong states that African biblical scholars must conceptualize our inherited images to communicate our answers.[5] Thus, an interpretation of the Nazareth maiden with African as the foreground becomes imperative. Furthermore, the 1993 Pontifical Biblical Commission document, "The Interpretation of the Bible in the Church" resonates with this manner of doing Scripture. The authority to write this book derives, in part, from this Pontifical Commission. The Commission urges women to engage actively in biblical interpretations to unearth the "feminine" face of the sacred text.

> Women have played a more active part in exegetical research. They have succeeded, often better than men, in detecting the presence, the significance, and the role of women in the Bible, in Christian origins, and in the Church. The world view of today, because of its greater attention to the dignity of women and to their role in society and in Church, ensures that new questions are put to the biblical text, which in turn occasions new discoveries. Feminine sensitivity helps to unmask and correct commonly accepted interpretations that were tendentious and sought to justify the male domination of women.[6]

It does appear that the commission gave women exegetes a *carte blanche* to explore the sacred text and to draw anew resources that speak to women's self-understanding, dignity and flourishing.

---

4. Boss, *Empress and Handmaid*, 12.

5. Ukpong, "New Testament Hermeneutics in Africa: Challenges and Possibilities," 158.

6. Béchard, "Scripture Documents," 272.

Investigating Mary's self-understanding in her assertion as *doulē kyriou*, the servant of the LORD, falls within the relationality and mutuality which characterizes most African societies as well as people of faith. To be in relationship suggests availability, and availability suggests service. To ground this undertaking in an African setting, we must establish some relationship.

Several reasons support employing the biblical text for advancing the cause of women, particularly in Africa: the place of the Bible in African thought, the role of the Bible in a globalized culture, and perhaps most importantly, the relationship of the land of the Bible with contemporary Africa. It would not be an overstatement to claim that neither political colonization nor globalization has succeeded in dismantling the authentic African cultural and religious practices. Rather, cultural revival in many African societies in recent times shows how deep-seated these values remain. I briefly explain each of the three points to enable the reader, particularly the non-African reader, to appreciate the interconnectedness of thoughts and religious expressions between Africa and the cultures that gave rise to biblical literature. This relationship, when fully explored, can lend support to a greater reception of the *doulē* metaphor for women, as well as men, in Africa and beyond.

The Bible and African Perspective

The Bible, the most influential book in the West, has been appropriated by Africans in a new way. The Botswana biblical scholar, Musa Dube, suggests that Africans' admission that they now have the Bible, implies that this text is no longer just a Western book.[7] Although evidence in the biblical text suggests that Africa has had the Bible in some fashion long before it became a Western book, one cannot ignore the place of the Bible in the contemporary African socio-cultural as well as religious context. Several scholars, Africans as well as non-Africans, attest to the current impact of the Bible on the continent.

The British scholar, Stephen Newell, articulated the currency of the biblical text in Nigeria and in other African sub-regions. For the many Christians in West Africa, the Bible offers spiritual enlightenment and practical guidance in daily life. In Nigeria, for example, ubiquitous preachers organize revivals on college campuses, tour public transporta-

---

7. Dube, *Postcolonial Feminist Interpretation*, 20.

tion facilities, and stand at street corners spreading the Gospel. These preachers and their collaborators distribute tracts and pamphlets to the general public.[8] For many contemporary Nigerian Christians, the Bible stands as a life-affirming text. But this life-affirming text also has served as a life-denying tool for many, particularly women. Asserting the negative use of the Bible, American scholar Clarice J. Martin echoes some biblical scholars, "The Bible has been used to curb women's movement toward full partnership in home, church, and society; to inhibit efforts to insure the more equitable distribution of power in societal institutions; and to discourage efforts to redefine and nurture more balanced and positive cultural images and roles of women."[9] Uncritical biblical reading continues to reflect negative images of women both religiously and socially. Scripture's influence on religious and social life makes it imperative to pay critical attention to the powerful rhetorical instruments of patriarchy, which marks a good part of the biblical text.

Roman Catholic teaching states that the Bible is inspired; because it is inspired, the Bible is the Word of God. This inspired writing, however, can best be interpreted by the believing communities, rather than by an isolated scholar bracketing any faith convictions.[10] Such collective interpretation makes the text become Scripture of the community. In other words, Scripture as the word of God becomes a community's frame of reference and functions normatively for the community of faith, providing inspiration in the ongoing articulation of a Christian self-understanding.[11]

The religious influence of the Bible is the second reason for employing the biblical text for advancing the cause of women. Religion exerts enormous influence on human endeavors. The practical problems confronting our world today cannot be adequately addressed without also considering important religious and ethical issues. That is because the way we think affects how we act; the way we feel immensely affects our perception and actions towards others.[12] Though sacred to only a small percentage of the human race, the Bible exerts enormous influence well beyond the confines of its adherents.

8. Newell, "Devotion and Domesticity," 296, 298.
9. Martin, "The *Haustafeln* (Household Codes)," 219.
10. Spohn, *Go and Do Likewise*, 22.
11. Schneiders, *Revelatory Text*, 64–93.
12. Spohn, *Go and Do Likewise*, 75–184.

Although African religious traditions differ in some aspects from the biblical traditions, similarities exist between contemporary African cultures and the culture of the land of the Bible on one hand, and meaning on the other. The degree of agreement in meanings lends itself to further exploration of the biblical text.

As for the the Hebrews of old, religion for most contemporary Africans is not a distinct aspect of culture. Religion is the horizon of everything else: politics, economics, social relations, law, medicine, ethics, and some other aspects of material culture as well. The current political landscape in many African countries is but an example of how these aspects of life intertwine. A few examples of cultural practices tend to corroborate some degree of affinity.

A striking similarity exists in the ideology that accompanies personal names. Most African names, like biblical names, have deeper meanings and can function as metaphors. I explain the significance of name in chapter 4. In addition, male circumcision eight days after birth, at least among the African-Igbo, confirms some likeness in both cultures.

Furthermore, in his autobiography, Olaudah Equiano, a freed slave, makes comparisons between his culture, which some scholars claim is Igbo, and the biblical laws.[13] Researchers assert that Olaudah Equiano was born *ca* 1745 in Igboland, and was captured and sold into slavery as a boy. When first introduced to the Bible in England, in 1759, Equiano, in his bewilderment wrote: "[I am] wonderfully surprised to see the laws and rules of my country written almost exactly here, a circumstance which I believe tended to impress our manners and customs more deeply on my memory."[14] Remarkably, Equiano's comment came some 120 years before the first Christian mission, the Church Mission Society, brought the Bible and Christianity to Igboland.

This paragraph owes to the work of Africa's foremost scholar of religion, John Mbiti. Mbiti pointed out that more than half of the Ten Commandments involve interpersonal relationship, a foundational mode of relationship in traditional African communities.[15] Furthermore, the attachment to the land represents an important issue for the African and the Hebrew. The land is thought of by both Africans and Israelites

---

13. Allison, *Interesting Narrative of the Life of Olaudah Equiano*.
14. Hastings, *The Church in Africa*, 328.
15. Mbiti, *Paths of African Theology*, 38.

as the basis of group consciousness.¹⁶ In addition a robust expression of interrelatedness goes beyond this life; the African tripartite notion of community that constitutes the living, the yet-to-be born, and the living-dead (ancestors) is replete in the Hebrew Scripture. Similarities exist also between many contemporary African women's religious practices and those of the ancient Hebrews.

Women's contemporary religious practices in many African societies corroborate the relationship. The tradition of household altars, preventative and restorative procedures in African culture, remain consistent with those of Israelite women of biblical times. The American scholar, Carol Myers, writing on women in ancient Israel states: "The rituals surrounding pregnancy, labor, and birth, along with those securing fertility before pregnancy and those dealing with postpartum lactation, infant care, and circumcision, constitute the religious culture of women more than men."¹⁷ These forms of practices and rituals are still practiced in many societies in contemporary sub-Saharan Africa, particularly in communities with minimal modern medical services.

African women theologians Mercy Amba Oduyoye and Musimbi Kanyaro, in *The Will to Arise*, point out that just as in Africa, the Bible privileges male value over female value.¹⁸ Infertility as a burden of women and the glorification of the birth of a male child are found in both cultures. This cultural affiliation confirms and provides a common ground for negotiating and appropriating biblical texts for transformative ends in Africa. In light of these findings, contemporary African women, would have little difficulty projecting their religious experience on to Mary of Nazareth, the *doulē kyriou*. These similarities in culture and meaning notwithstanding, there exists fundamental difficulty in current biblical interpretation in Africa.

In addition, the Nigerian exegete, David Tuesday Adamo, supports the assertion of resemblance between the culture of the land of the Bible and Africa from ancient historical sources. His sources include the works of Diodorus Cicilus, Plutarch, Flavius Josephus, Celsus, Tacitus, and Eusebius.¹⁹ Adamo contends that many ancient historians believe that the original Hebrews included Ethiopians and Egyptians, who were

16. Mbiti, *Paths of African Theology*, 38.
17. Myers, *Households and Holiness*, 17.
18. Oduyoye and Kanyoro, *Will to Arise*, 4.
19. Adamo, *Africans in the New Testament*, 22.

forced to migrate to Canaan. He grounds his argument by contrasting the seventy souls (Gen. 46:27) that came to North African Egypt with the six hundred thousand souls (Exod 12:37) that left Egypt after four hundred and thirty years (Exod 12:40). Adamo insists that with the policy of intermarriage in Africa, if the Hebrew clan, were white when they entered Egypt and stayed for 430 years, they would probably have been considerably black by the time they left Egypt.[20] Moreover, Exodus 12:38 reports that those who left Egypt with the Hebrews were a mixed multitude, "A crowd of mixed ancestry," which may also include Asians (Exod 12: 37–38). These facts lend support to the African influence on the Hebrew worldview. A critical study of these similarities may yield a better understanding, as well as facilitate appropriation of the biblical text in contemporary Africa.

Interpretation and appropriation of the biblical text in contemporary Africa is fraught with dangers. Fundamentalism represents one such danger. Fundamentalism, which represents radicalism in its deepest expression, insists that it reproduces and makes normative, for the contemporary period, what it perceives as biblical-era beliefs and practices.[21] This attitude that stresses strict and literal adherence to a set of basic principles is becoming a growing concern in many African Christian communities for Catholics and Protestants alike. A fundamentalist approach to a biblical interpretation discounts the fact that biblical truths cannot be prepackaged. It fails to recognize that truth must be found in interaction between text and context in the actual historical circumstances. Christian fundamentalism, as a powerful rhetorical instrument of patriarchy tends to impose literal biblical text, particularly where it reinforces women's subjugation.[22] Thus, the movement poses a threat to uncovering and reclaiming liberative concepts lost or systematically suppressed by androcentric translations and interpretations. The Nigerian scholar of religion, Ogbu U. Kalu, summed up fundamentalist attitudes among Evangelical and Pentecostal movements, "There is a basket of ironies: evangelical and charismatic spirituality feed on the freedom of Christ, but breed conservative ethics, Biblicism, and the canonization of select Pauline 'verses of terror,' family values, and the submission of

---

20. Adamo, *Africans in the New Testament*, 22.

21. Marty, "Fundamentalism as a Social Phenomenon," 19–29. See, also Harrington David Watt, "The Meaning and End of Fundamentalism," 269–73.

22. Donaldson, "The Sign of Orpah: Reading Ruth through Native Eyes," 36.

women. Even the Promise Keepers (a movement begun in the United States) of our times are alleged to have become a bastion of male chauvinist effort to restore non-liberal values about the status of women."[23] A radical fundamentalist reading of the biblical texts reinforces oppressive structures.

Fundamentalism suppresses and hinders the women's effort in working towards greater participation in social and church life.

Biblical interpretation represents not just religious discourse for and among Christians. Meanings derived from biblical interpretations also can influence public and political discourse. The so-called women's place in society and church life is in part reinforced by such interpretations. On this basis, the use of the biblical text becomes crucial in reimagining and redreaming women's role in society and church life.

The Handmaid: Ecclesial Appropriation

The Handmaid in this section of our discussion represents women who have taken the vows of religion. An understanding of Mary of Nazareth in the ecclesial community varies, but two levels stand out: the relationship dictated by patriarchal ecclesiastical structures, and the level to which the sisters accept this oversight, which labels them servile.

At the first level, some ecclesial communities are ambiguous about the Sisters' role in the church and society. There seems to be an understanding that women religious are measured against the standard of Mary the "submissive maiden" of Nazareth. Perhaps that notion gave rise to the given names of Sisters, names prefixed by "Mary" such as Sister Mary Beatrice, Sister Maria Goretti, or Marie Thérèse, in the pre-Vatican Church.

The understanding of Mary as maidservant in religious circles, particularly within the ecclesial community, has gained currency as emblematic of the biblical handmaid in the sense of *paidiskē*.[24] *Paidiskē* is a name given to female servile, or, in literal translation, servile women, a designation that denotes one under tutelage, an appendage, and one socially underage. Moreover, *paidiskē* exists in contradistinction to *doulē*. *Doulē* is a self-designated name of leading biblical women, a notion which I explore further in the next chapter.

---

23. Kalu, "Daughters of Ethiopia: Constructing a Feminist Discourse in Ebony Strokes," 272.

24. Buhner, "*Paidiskē*," 5.

Seeing Mary as a maidservant plays a significant role in the self-understanding of religious Sisters. Many women have allowed this image of Mary to determine their engagement with life. This has proved to be rather non-liberating. Rather than being a liberative model for the Sisters, the image of Mary so strongly connected to their religious beliefs tends to further domesticate them. In some instances, the religious vow of obedience is tied to Mary's *fiat*. Sisters are urged to obey promptly "like Mary!" They are never to ask questions. This understanding of "prompt" obedience grossly undermines the dialogical relationship represented in the drama of the annunciation. How can anyone overlook the fact that it is in dialogue that the "Word became Flesh?" Undoubtedly, the slave-master mentality these women have appropriated can pave the way for fideism. In other words, the attitude becomes whatever they say/decide that I will do, God will take care! They, in this sense, mean those in authority. Ironically, the community itself ceases to exist in the proper sense of the word when Sisters can no longer make informed decisions about their lives. To forestall this dismal situation, it becomes imperative for the believing community to actively and collectively engage in interpreting this inspired Word of God for it to truly become life-giving, the Word of life. Although the enduring reading of Handmaid as model of subservience has gained ground, evidence shows that a careful reading of the Lukan narrative (1:26–38), suggests otherwise.

The Handmaid: A Contemporary Understanding

The paucity of literature on the word "handmaid" hinders extensive study of the term. Moreover, materials on the biblical handmaid *per se* are almost non-existent. In this case, context lends itself to interpretation. Given the poverty of biblical resources, Apocryphal texts have been employed to augment understanding of "handmaid."

The English meaning of handmaiden does not support the term as equivalent to slavery, but rather as a woman serving as an attendant, a girl servant or a useful subordinate, but never a subject. Materials from both the Hebrew Scripture and the Greek Septuagint show that the word "handmaid" is multi-layered, suggesting its metaphorical usage.

The metaphoric use of the term allowed Christians over the centuries to interpret Mary's relationship to God in a variety of different ways. Sarah Jane Boss demonstrates the historical correlations between understanding of the Handmaid and cultural changes.[25] Boss' assertion suggests that the image of Mary of Nazareth is not fixed. Mary's image is being constantly rewoven to meet the spiritual needs of the times. It could be argued that the phenomenon of Our Lady of Guadalupe represents one such reweaving for the Mexicans. However, the experience of Mary in Africa remains stagnant. In African Christianity, the images of Mary as Virgin and as Mother dominate the Marian landscape. Introduced by missionaries several centuries ago, the image of Mary has not gone beyond the devotional circle. Some of these spiritual practices subliminally reinforce the submissive and passive nature attributed to Mary of Nazareth, sustaining women's subordination. Because women's spiritual practices consist mostly of Marian spirituality, they find themselves locked-down in this devotion that tends to domesticate. Furthermore, certain expressions of Mary in Igbo milieu, for example, mirror her as a shadowy figure. The designation, *nwa Nmeri*, (*nwa* = a child; *Nmeri* = Mary), meaning a child of Mary, represents one such expression. *Nwa Nmeri* can sometimes mean a favorable expression that designates a pious person, male or female. But the name can take on a different meaning when deliberately applied to a female. When a female, regardless of age, is called *nwa Nmeri*, it usually and pejoratively would mean an unsophisticated person or a person innocently naïve. A deeper meaning of such ascription does not suggest a liberative image of Mary.

The subdued image of Mary translates into much of contemporary Christian art. The Filipina Benedictine, Mary John Manazan, captured some contemporary depiction of Mary thus, in "The Blessed Virgin who is presented as a model for the woman is often portrayed as a passive and submissive plaster saint instead of the valiant woman in the Bible who sang the strong verses of the Magnificat and stood courageously at the foot of the cross."[26] Very few paintings of the Annunciation project the image of Mary as one who possesses agency. Recent historical understandings of the "handmaid" portray her as ever meek and unassuming, one devoid of passion, waiting to be led. The contrast between the biblical Mary and the exegetical Mary is clear, demonstrated in several vernacular representations.

---

25. Boss, *Empress and Handmaid*, 12.
26. Mananzan, "Education to Femininity or Education to Feminism," 190.

In similar vein, the Mexican-American theologian, Nora Lozano-Vinz, claims that the characteristics assigned to our Lady of Guadalupe are not very liberating. For in the Mexican and Mexican-American tradition, Guadalupe represents "a saintly woman who has embodied attributes such as virginity, piety, helplessness, forgiveness, goodness, and devoted and selfless motherhood."[27] However, Lozano-Vinz's reading of the Virgin of Guadalupe undermines upholding the Virgin's cosmological embrace of humanity, and the hope of a poor person in the face of ecclesiastical domination. Interpretations such as Lozano-Vinz's fall short of capturing the expression of servant and leader of the new People of God, which the Lukan *doulē kyriou* signifies.

In addition, other texts of twentieth-century devotion tend to support this notion of Mary's position as that of servile woman. Insights from the Nigerian scholar, Becky Iwuchukwu, represent one such text. "Mary showed deep faith in God, and complete obedience to the divine will. The African woman will also learn from Mary how and when to be silent, obedient to her husband and always very ready to make the sacrifices demanded by one that has answered God's call."[28] Iwuchukwu's reading of the Mary in Luke 1:38 distorts the significance of the event. The interpretation she offers reinforces the ideology of subordination. Such understanding represents the enduring perception that Mary's passive humility fits her for the role of the Mother of the Redeemer. The insistence on subordination of wives and unguided sacrifice represents the most silencing factor for the African woman. To redeem this situation, some African feminist scholars, drawing from the Lukan narrative, propose Mary's motherhood as metaphor for women's advancement.

The Handmaid: an African Adaptation

The narrative of Luke 1:26–38 is a liberative story. The centrality of a female character in this passage represents not only a birth narrative but a story of liberation. When viewed primarily as a birth narrative, the discussion becomes complicated and can jeopardize women's advancement. But for some African feminist scholars, this Lukan passage mediates human promotion by virtue of its being a birth narrative.[29] The

27. Lozano-Díaz, "Ignored Virgin or Unaware Women," 210.

28. Iwuchukwu, "Women and Religion in Africa," 47.

29. Okure, "A New Testament Perspective on Evangelization and Human Promotion," 128.

reason for this assertion is it glorifies motherhood, particularly in a biological sense. The concept of motherhood is problematic. Motherhood means different things to different people. Although the full semantic range of both the literal and metaphorical meaning of motherhood cannot be achieved in this discussion, I show motherhood to constitute service. Motherhood is about servanthood; a servant always on duty, always thinking about how to build up the family, the community and bring beauty to life. From the experience of service as mothers, women move to the experience of community, burst the confining limits of their domestic tasks and discover themselves as creators of history. In this way, motherhood valorizes and can become liberative. In other words, motherhood reveals actions or events that unburden, lift up, or promote the humanity of persons, individuals and collective groups.

Motherhood is glorious; however, the disproportionate emphasis placed on motherhood in the biological sense proves limiting and oppressive to women who cannot be biological mothers. Even if the concept of motherhood includes an understanding that the status of mother is not totally dependent on biological functions, the dominant notion of the term is primarily tied to giving birth. Mary's motherhood in the annunciation context is not philosophical; it is about the fruit of her womb: biology (Luke 1:31). The Nigerian scholar, Oyeronke Olajubu expresses dissatisfaction with the motherhood metaphor for women's advancement. She rejects the metaphor because the underlying factor that supports such idea derives from a woman's sexual and reproductive status.[30] The prominence given to motherhood in the annunciation narrative raises difficulties and challenges the engaged reader to find new metaphors that would be liberative. I argue that Mary's self-understanding as the servant of the LORD, *doulē kyriou*, represents one such new metaphor. This metaphor confronts the views of African feminist scholars who assert "motherhood as the key metaphor for the wise and good women in Africa."[31] In support of this argument, the Kenyan feminist scholar, Anne Nasimiyu Wasike, states that "in African traditional societies, women and girls were never killed during a war because they carried within them the future generations."[32] This understanding implied that killing women and girls leads to self-extinction.

30. Olajubu, *Women in the Yoruba Religious Sphere*, 94.
31. Pemberton, ed., *Circle Thinking*, 106.
32. Nasimiyu-Wasike, "Jesus: An African perspective," 331.

Paradoxically, the same tradition, which protects women and girls, perpetuates a life-denying system that prevents them from realizing their full potential in society. In this light, the protection given to women and girls seems to suggest mere utilitarian gesture. Women who subscribe to the motherhood metaphor draw support from androcentric wisdom corpus. This body of writings and thoughts consistently highlights the elevated position of the mother who is accorded esteem and respect.[33] In other words, for women, motherhood becomes an avenue for power. This stance resonates with a saying from William Ross Wallace's 1865 poem titled "What Rules the World: The Hand That Rocks the Cradle Is the Hand That Rules the World."

But motherhood in itself does not represent power. Drawing from the Lukan narrative, motherhood for Mary does not pose a position of power. Rather, motherhood constitutes service. One can interpret the immediate sequence of events that follows angel Gabriel's announcement thus: On receiving power from the Spirit to bear the Incarnate Word, Mary went with haste to serve in the home of Elizabeth and Zachariah (Luke 1:39ff). The sense of power in itself is antithetical to the very concept of the Servant of the LORD.

On the other hand, a metaphorical reading of motherhood is inclusive and can be liberating. Metaphorical motherhood can be defined as mother without child. Images of metaphorical motherhood abound in the Scripture. Fourth Ezra, a Jewish apocalypse written near the end of the first century C.E., for example, employs mother earth as a conceptual framework. In Igbo tradition, *Ala*, the earth Goddess is represented as mother. Do these ideas not resonate with the time-tested parlance of motherland? Thus motherhood in this broader sense is within the reach of everyone, women as well as men. In his first letter to the Thessalonians, the apostle Paul represents himself in a gynomorphic image. Paul compares himself to a mother, who nurses his children: "Rather we were gentle among you, as a nursing mother cares for her children. With such affection for you, we were determined to share with you not only the gospel of God, but our very selves as well (I Thess 2:7b–8)." Thus motherhood can be an universal image that expresses service. Service can be expressed in a regeneration of life through nurturing. One must also take notice of another category of motherhood, the Desert Mothers,

---

33. Schottroff, et al., *Feminist Interpretation*, 125.

ammas, of early Christianity and the contemporary Reverend Mothers of monasteries and convents.

Curiously, most women desire not just biological motherhood but a male-child. A contextual reading of these motherhood-male-child passages in the biblical texts reveals several socio-cultural issues. In ancient Jewish society, for example, a female is a nonentity. For the people of those days, a female is of consequence only in relation to a male relative: her father, husband, or son. Biblical birth narratives that applaud the birth of sons reinforce the fact that daughters are of little significance to that culture. These underlying factors made it imperative for women to become not just mothers but bearers of sons. Do those passages represent contemporary situations? Today's social context demands a re-reading of those passages that devalue the female by elevating the male and employing same in furthering women's advancement. Such reading takes into consideration that the Bible represents a product of human culture with its ideologies, worldviews and orientation, perspectives, values and disvalues.

The Roman Catholic tradition teaching on Mariology and female empowerment indicates that motherhood does not always lead to empowerment.[34] Had motherhood translated to a liberative empowerment, Mary's motherhood would have assuaged the quandary surrounding gender roles, at least in Church life. However, the Lukan passage under study persistently makes clear that motherhood, as Mary of Nazareth embraces it, can be a liberating concept, if viewed in terms of service, relationality and mutuality. But, a woman's rootedness as one in the Lord's service, the *doulē*, prepares her to face the world as a human person fully alive. Therefore, when women continue to place procreation at the center of their universe, they inadvertently perpetuate their own oppression by accepting "malestream" categories.[35] "Malestream" is a feminist term in contradistinction to mainstream.

Feminists' scholars who continue to claim motherhood as a source of power play into the malestream thought. Moreover, some women scholars perpetuate the teachings from certain biblical passages that privileges motherhood as social security for women. The American scholar Kathleen S. Nash states, "The ideas that many children are a blessing and that woman's self-importance derives from giving birth are

---

34. Schottroff, et al., *Feminist Interpretation*.
35. Oduyoye and Kanyoro, *Will to Arise*, 17.

cultural constructs designed to encourage large families that promote agricultural prosperity, to ensure social prestige for the fathers, and to divert feminine energy into maintaining a patriarchal structure whose margins house women and their children."[36] Nash further argues that the desire for motherhood stems from male narrators who define motherhood as the social role that brings women honor and happiness. Such representations of women "disregard…the possibility that women might object to risking their life repeatedly in pregnancy and childbirth."[37] Women who posit motherhood as metaphor for women's advancement run the risk of exposing women to untimely death. These pitfalls make it obvious that the motherhood metaphor does not promote the feminist discourse.

Furthermore, being a woman is not explicitly fixed by the created order in her role as mother. Yet, women's continual insistence on maternity as preeminent raises a fundamental question of the female identity. Women, who take such a position, further implicate themselves in their own subordination. Olajubu gives an example of the unconstructive implications the privileging of motherhood can have on a Nigerian-Yoruba woman, "For one, the inability to become a mother could begin a traumatic process of alienation and frustration for the Yoruba woman. She is perceived as a dead end through whom the ancestral line cannot continue and this could translate to ridicule in the society."[38] Women more than men, are likely to suffer indignity as a result of their inability to beget biological children. The humiliation and mortification in itself represents a silencing mechanism, life-denying circumstance and as such does not lead one to live, share and enjoy life to the fullest with others.

In addition, the American theologian, Elisabeth Schüsler Fiorenza, aptly states that biological motherhood is not enjoined on women. Rather, women like men, are called to faithful discipleship.[39] Fiorenza insists that the truly 'great' are those who become servants or slave, *doulas, douloi*.[40] Mary of Nazareth is not blessed because of her being Jesus' biological mother (Luke 11:27). Blessedness arises, according to Jesus, by

---

36. Nash, "Mother," 923.
37. Nash, "Mother," 923.
38. Olajubu, *Women in the Yoruba*, 17.
39. Schüsler Fiorenza, *In Memory of Her*, 146.
40. Schüsler Fiorenza, 148.

hearing God's word and observing it. "Rather blessed are those who hear the word of God and keep it" (Luke 11:28). Jesus' declaration evidently subverts biological motherhood as a suitable definition for womanhood in the Christian community. Mary of Nazareth as a symbol of womanhood in Christianity, models for people of faith a way of being related to God and to humankind: to serve the Word.

Moreover, the Gospel according to Luke situates Jesus' overall mission in the context of service "For who is greater: the one seated at table or the one who serves? Is it not the one seated at table? I am among you as the one who serves" (Luke 22:27). Jesus in the Gospel reminds his disciples, and by extension us, that greatness is tied to our willingness to be servants and not to be served. Service constitutes the quintessential quality of the *Doulē*, a characteristic, which distinguishes people of faith and culture. Mary of Nazareth in her position as *doulē kyriou*, therefore, can become a model of self-identification for women in their engagement with society and church life.

The above excursus, designed to bring into the conversation the different thoughts and scenario in which the Handmaid is envisioned, prepares the reader to engage the *doul*-stem word in its metaphoric usage in the next chapter.

2

Handmaid: the *Doulē* and Israel's *Doulas* Figures

"Without women 'a lineage is finished'"[1]

MERCY AMBA ODUYOYE

Introduction

SCRIPTURE CONTINUES TO BE a significant source and origin of religious and social attitudes about gender, race/ethnicity class and colonialism. Uncritical use of Bible stories has often legitimized the subjugation of women, either by omitting stories about women or through gender-biased interpretation. The role Scripture plays in social processes makes it a crucial resource for women's advancement projects. As a means for identity construction, Scriptural narratives provide the woof and weft with which to weave an understanding that speaks positively of women in society and Church life. Because a people remain as healthy and as confident as the stories they tell, retelling the stories of heroic women in Scripture provides models of positive self-identification, for women in contemporary society and church life.

The history and construction of identity constitutes the key categories of my interests in understanding the "Handmaid." Constructing a theology of positive self-identification, therefore, benefits from a plurality of voices when experiences are reread from broader templates. This narrative plumbs the biblical tradition to access the plurality of voices that speak of the *doulē*.

A limited source of information on Mary the mother of Jesus is found in the fourfold Gospel. Canadian biblical scholar Lawrence Frizzell

---

1. Oduyoye, *Daughters of Anowa*, 7.

noted that since the fourfold Gospel offers only a limited source that features Mary, the mother of Jesus, the great doctors of the early Church and the theologians of the Middle Ages found abundant resources for their meditation concerning Mary in the Jewish Scriptures and literature related to the New Testament.[2] Jewish Scriptures, the Septuagint, and Deuterocanonical resources contain women's stories that support and sustain the image of the Lukan *doulē kyriou* in the sense of servant leader. American scholar John Drury notes Luke's extensive use of material from the Septuagint, "It is not just the pace and the prologue that derives from the ancient Scripture. So do the language, characters, and actual events. The language imitates the Septuagint and is full of its stock phrases."[3] The Conciliar document, particularly *Dei Verbium* (#11) also notes of the use of Scripture and tradition in bringing the role of Mary into a "gradually clearer light." The slave designation, which the English interpretation of "Handmaid" renders, however, conceals more than it reveals about Mary. Dismantling that which cloaks the true nature of Mary, and bringing to light this servant leader, represents the interest underlying my story, *Handmaid: The Power of Names in Theology and Society*.

This chapter examines the *doulē* term. The discussion further reveals how certain Hebrew women embody the understanding of Handmaid in the sense of *doulē*. The Hebraic understanding is distinguished from the common understanding of handmaid as slave or indentured servant. The biblical characters of Ruth, Abigail, Esther, and Judith provide the examples that ground my thought.

A HEBRAIC UNDERSTANDING OF THE TERMS `EBED, DOULĒ, PAIDISKĒ

The Greek term with the *doul*-stem, from which derives the expression Handmaid, also denotes slave. The use of the term in the Septuagint, however, strongly suggests the Hebraic sense of the word `ebed.[4] The Septuagint (LXX) was the first authorized translation of the Hebrew Scriptures into Greek, brought to us by the Alexandrian library and the

---

2. Frizzell, "Mary and the Biblical Heritage," 26.
3. Drury, "Luke," 419.
4. Weiser, *Exegetical Dictionary of the New Testament*, vol. 1, p'Aarwn i'Enwc, 347–48.

captive Jews, seventy elders, who performed it. I recite these well-known facts because they were slaves who outwitted their captors by agreeing with each other, if the Letter of Aristeas is in any way credible. In the Hebrew sense, however, the seventy elders were `ebed, in service of the community. Hebrew `ebed describes prophets, rulers and, holy persons as servants or slaves of God. Given the atrocious history of slavery, some may find the term *doulē*/slave an unacceptable redemptive vehicle. Perhaps the use of the term "handmaid" mitigates the caustic language of slave, which the *doul*-stem word denotes. However, experience shows that changing problematic words never produces lasting solutions. This narrative gives an imaginative explanation of the vexing terminology, a term that is rooted in service and leadership. The conclusion shows that the metaphor of the *doulē* signifies positive retrieval and provides a key, one which can unlock and make possible a liberative future of abundant life, not only for women but for men as well. At this point, some word study will enhance the understanding of the *doulē* term.

Word Study: Doul-stem

The *doul*-stem word in the Septuagint [LXX] connects two other words, `ebed and *pais*.[5] However, `abadim in its basic biblical meaning represents `ebed, someone in a subservient relationship to another, a relationship that is not necessarily of ownership. Of all the slave-designate terms, *doulos/doulē, oiketés, therapón, andrapodon soma, aichmalótos, and pais*, the Septuagint designates female slaves most often by *doulē, paidiskē, therapaina*, and *korasion*.[6] These variants provide pertinent information that suggests metaphorical usage.[7] The metaphoric usage of the slave-designate word *doulē* is lost in the English translation "handmaid." But various applications of the *doul*-stem word make evident the slave/free contrast. A brief survey of the term *pais, paidiskē*, illumines its meaning and shades light on the significance of the *doulos/doulē* term.

Pais derives roots in *paidia*, meaning a child and one under tutelage. *Pais/paidiskē* also can mean a young slave/servant (slave of God). Abraham calls Hagar *paidiskē*, acknowledging her to be a child and a

---

5. Buhner, *Exegetical Dictionary of the New Testament*, volume 3, *pagideuw–wfelimos*, 5. See, also De Swarte Gilfford, "American Women and the Bible," 19.

6. Balz, and Radi, *Exegetical Dictionary*, Vol., 2, 308, 479. See, also J. A. Fitzmer, *Exegetical Dictionary*, Vol., 3, 39–40.

7. Wright, "`Ebed/Doulos" 85.

slave (Gen 16:6). The LXX renders *'ebed* as *pais*, although *'ebed* does not indicate slave status in the absolute, but subservient status vis-à-vis someone or something else.[8] Absolute slavery consists in the disempowerment of the subject and in the radical loss of control of one's personhood.

The *paidiskē*, that is, the slave women, has no social status. She is frequently not named. Thus one named *paidiskē* has neither voice nor agency. A *paidiskē* constitutes the personal property of a specific person. In Genesis 20:14; 24:35, the use of *paidiskē* indicates the acquisition of women as property. The *paidiskē* could be a concubine, as in the case of Sarah and Hagar or Rachel and Bilhah. When Rachel failed to bear children, she gave her *paidiskē*, Bilhah, to Jacob so that through her, she, Rachel might be a mother (Gen 30: 1– 8). Had Luke cast his maiden from Nazareth in the role of *paidiskē* (Luke 1: 26–38) the question of Mary's slave status would be unquestionable. Literature of a later Greek period, however, utilizes both *doulos* and *pais* to render the word *'ebed*.

Doul-stem Word in Hebraic Tradition

Biblical scholars posit that the Hebraic usage of the *doul*-stem word applies to outstanding men and women in Israel's history. These include Abraham, Isaac, Moses, Joshua, Ruth, Hannah, David, Solomon, Esther, Judith, and a few others. These men and women at one time or another addressed themselves "as slave of God" (*douloi, doulas*).

At different times in Israel's history, the term *'ebed* or *doulos* of Yahweh, came to represent God's servants. *Doulos kyriou* describes Joshua (24:30). David calls himself *doulos* in a passage where he clearly is volunteering to enter the service of the king (cf. 1Sam 17:32). At least five Hebrew words, *amah*, *shiphchah*, *bethulah*, *almah*, and *naarah* all are translated as "handmaid" in English.[9] Of significance are the terms *amah* and *shiphchah*. While the Hebrew Scripture employs the term *amah* to describe the devout and pious woman, it reserves the term *shiphchah* for female slaves (Gen 24:35; 30:43).[10] It is significant that the Septuagint consistently renders as *amah*, *doulē* and *shiphchah*, *paidiskē*. Even within English translation, the common usage of handmaiden does not support

---

8. Rengstorf, "Slave-*doulos*," 183.
9. Carr, "Maid, Maiden," 1379–1380.
10. Carr, "Maid, Maiden," 1379–1380.

the term as equivalent to slavery, but rather as a woman serving as an attendant, a girl servant or a useful subordinate. The occurrences of the word handmaid in the English Bible show that not all handmaidens were chattel slaves or servile.

Doul-stem word in Ancient Literature

*Doul-*stem words represent one of many nouns used to designate a slave during the Hellenistic-Roman period. *Doulos/doulē* usage in the Septuagint (LXX) emerges from a confluence of ideas and circumstances found in the culture of the ancient Near East from which Israel received, in part, its cultural self-definition. A. Weiser stated that in the Hebrew Scriptures and in Judaism, *doul-*stem word has a different meaning from its Hellenistic usage, "A totally different understanding is expressed in the OT and in Judaism: God is the absolute Lord. The individual knows that he is dependent on God. To be chosen by God, to be able to serve him, is not demeaning; on the contrary, it is an honor. Consequently words of the *doul-*stem in the LXX are most frequently translated equivalents for the root *'bd* [servant of God] and its denominative."[11]

The LXX renders *douleuein* the most common term for the service of God, not just in isolated acts, but in total commitment. Other scholars commented that in the LXX, the word *doulos* denotes not only slave of human masters, but also designates the pious and the faithful, especially prophets and rulers (cf. 2 Kgs 16:7; 2 Sam 10:19; 2 Kgs 18:24).[12] Terms such as *doulos/doulē theou*, signify a humble self-deprecation before a superior, especially before God. A clear distinction exists between the Hebrew *'ebed* in ancient Israel and *'ebed* among non-Jews. The Hebrew *'ebed* in many respects implies a debt-slave or an indentured servant.

*Doul-*stem words function in manners in which even the highest officials are *doulos,* slaves, before their king. American scholar Benjamin Wright, among other biblical scholars identified the use of the term *doulos,* representing "slave of God" as perhaps an idea unique to the Jews and their scriptural traditions. The notion of *doulos* as slave of God resonates with Israel's self-conception as a nation of people who represent "servants of God," as opposed to servants of human rulers.[13]

---

11. Rengstorf, "Slave-*doulos*, 184.
12. Rengstorf, "Slave-*doulos*, 184.
13. Wright, "'Ebed/Doulos," 109.

Besides, Diaspora Jews had to contend with transforming their notion of *doulos* from that of the Hebrew world to that of the slave systems in their new surrounding, "The term *doulos*, one of the two major translations of `*ebed* in the Jewish-Greek Bible, quite simply communicated to the Greek reader in this period something different from what the word `*ebed* did earlier. The consideration most probably applies not only to those instances in which an actual servant or slave is meant, but also to metaphorical uses of the terminology."[14]

In a Hellenistic sense, *doul*-stem word emphatically denotes the slave and the status of slavery. In some sense, however, the Hebrew `*ebed* and Greek *doulos* overlap and each covers a wide range of semantic domains that name a variety of inferiors and are often nontechnical in ancient vernacular.[15]

Several sources support the polyvalent use of the *doul*-stem word. Evidence from the Septuagint and literature from the Second Temple period favor Hebrew `*ebed* translation into *doulos*. Ancient authors, such as Josephus and Philo of Alexandria employ the *doul*-stem word metaphorically. For Josephus a *doulos* means a chattel slave; to be a *doulos* means to lose all of one's freedoms.[16] But scholars such as Wright note that Josephus' exclusive designation of *doulos* arises because he did not carefully distinguish among his words for slaves, generally using them as synonyms.[17] Josephus at some point in his career was enslaved by the Roman government as a political prisoner. Possibly this experience of being fettered influenced his rendering of the *doul*-stem word.

The writings of Philo of Alexandria also show a wide vocabulary of the *doul*-word. Philo mostly utilized slave terms philosophically and metaphorically. Philo posits that one can be enslaved to one's desires, passions, emotions, or appetites.[18] *Doulos*, therefore, represents the state of loss; an absolute loss of personal freedom and being controlled by personal desires. Philo does acknowledge that the term *doulos* can also mean service. He utilizes *doulos* and *therapón* to designate slave of God in the Hebriac sense. Philo presupposes that a statesman's service to the state is like that of a *doulos*. According to Wright, in many instances

14. Wright, "`Ebed/Doulos," 84.
15. Harrill, "Servant," 1189.
16. Wright, "`Ebed/Doulos," 98.
17. Wright, "`Ebed/Doulos."
18. Wright, "`Ebed/Doulos."

Philo changed the Septuagint use of *pais* to *doulos*, which suggests their contemporary Hellenistic Greek usage. Like Josephus, Philo's use of synonyms of Hellenistic slave terms crowds out specific meaning of *doul*-stem word. In this regard, a more approximate meaning of *doul*-stem word resides in context. Extant ancient literatures suggest that the main terms for slaves roughly can be synonymous.

Doul-stem Word in the New Testament

In the era of the New Testament, a slave's influence was determined by the owner's social position. Imperial slaves wielded more power than ordinary slaves. Those who claimed to be slaves of God possessed even greater influence. Thus the apostle Paul frequently refers to himself as slave, *doulos*, of Christ. In a similar sense Mary of Nazareth addresses herself as *doulē kyriou*. Paul's self-designation, God's *doulos*, reflects not only his understanding of the serving nature of his apostolate, but also shows his privileged status as an apostle of the only one master, Christ, whom Paul serves in other people (2 Cor 4: 5). The Book of Revelation even presents Moses as *doulos* (Rev 15:3).

Generally, the New Testament use of the *doul*-stem word portrays less than a positive image. *Doul*-stem word in the New Testament, with very few exceptions, denote almost exclusively a demeaning, scornful significance. New Testament *doulē* translates almost totally, handmaid, maidservant or slave. The *doul*-stem word, expresses slavery to matter and to the world powers, a notion consistent with the Greco-Roman world where the service of slaves lacked dignity unless it was service to the state. The ethos of Luke-Acts and its application of the *doul*-stem word, however, offer bold suggestions about how the church must understand itself and order its faith. Hence, the *doulē* or *doulas* in Luke-Acts bear the family resemblance of the Hebrew `ebed in its usage. Raymond Brown echoed a similar idea. He traced the Lukan *doulē* back to its Septuagint use. Brown insists that because Luke describes most of the adult figures of the infancy narrative against the Hebrew Scripture background, it would be surprising if he did not place Mary against this background as well.[19] Moreover, the author of Luke is aware that history flows out of the Old Testament's Jewish past into the Christian future. Thus he begins his narrative with the barren, childless parents of Jesus' herald, John

---

19. Brown, et al., 34. See, also McLay, *The Use of the Septuagint*, 30.

the Baptist. "His characters are revivals of old Jewish types. Elizabeth and Zacharias are 'righteous before God' like Noah, childless Abraham and Sarah. Mary greets Elizabeth with an 'occasional poem' very closely modeled on Hannah's (Luke 1:46–55; I Sam 2:1–11)."[20] Luke's positioning of Mary alongside figures from the past casts her in the tradition of Israel's heroine; savior figures that made God's work come true in Israel. Thus Mary of Nazareth is ranked with Israel's *doulas*; an arrangement that befits her role as the mother of the Savior. Israel's *doulas* represent faithful, wise and, courageous women who enabled God's salvation plan to happen in Israel's history (cf. Matt 1:5–6).

Tested against the evidence of the ancient texts, Mary's self description as *doulē*, places her more in the tradition of Israel's savior figures than in the Greco-Roman concept of the *doul*-stem word. Regrettably, the dominant version of the *doul*-stem word in the New Testament, subverts the meaning of Luke's *doulē kyriou* in Luke 1:26–38.

Doul-stem Word in Christian Arts and Literature

The subdued image of the *doul*-stem word finds its way into much of contemporary Christian art and literature. Some paintings of the Annunciation scene depict the "handmaid" in an utterly subservient manner, portraying her more as a *paidiskē* than a *doulē*. Evidently these depictions do not convey the biblical portrayal of Mary in her self-assertion as the *doulē kyriou* in Luke 1:26–38. Several feminist scholars speak of the unconstructive effect the portrayal of Mary as subservient has on women in general. Among these scholars is a Filipina Benedictine, Mary John Manazan. Sister Mary John Manazen captured some contemporary depiction of Mary of Nazareth already cited earlier.

Very few contemporary arts thus present Mary as one with agency. Recent historical understanding of the Handmaid portrays her as ever meek and unassuming, one devoid of passion, waiting to be led. Texts of twentieth-century devotion tend to support the idea as well. The Nigerian scholar, Becky Iwuchukwu seems to favor such text. Iwuchukwu's reading of Mary in the Annunciation represents a misreading of the significance of the event. Chapter 3 will explore further the implications of Mary's "silence" and the liberating echoes that voicing represents. We

---

20. Drury, "Luke," 419.

also shall see that her acclaimed obedience derives primarily from her celebrated silence.

Iwuchukwu's interpretation represents the enduring reception that Mary's passive humility, rather than her character and ability, fit her for the role of the Mother of the Redeemer. Such rendering of the passage reinforces the ideology of subordination. The insistence on subordination of wives and unguided sacrifice constitutes the most silencing factor. Iwuchukwu's sense of women's role affects contemporary women's experience in Igbo society. Such socialization forced the majority of women to accept the subsidiary and complementary roles reserved for them in Igbo Westernized society and church life.

Iwuchukwu's interpretation represents the enduring reception that Mary's passive humility, rather than her character and ability, fit her for the role of the Mother of the Redeemer. Such rendering of the passage reinforces the ideology of subordination. The insistence on subordination of wives and unguided sacrifice constitutes the most silencing factor. Iwuchukwu's sense of women's role affects contemporary women's experience in Igbo society. Such socialization forced the majority of women to accept the subsidiary and complementary roles reserved for them in Igbo Westernized society and church life. Iwuchukwu's reading and the aforementioned insight of Nora Lozano-Vinz on the Lady of Guadalupe,[21] defeats the biblical witness of an all-powerful liberating God, whose concern for the ultimate and holistic liberation of all humanity began with a young Nazarene maiden. Texts such as these fall short of capturing the expression of servant-leader, which the *doulē* signifies.

Doul-stem Word in Igbo Tradition

Igbo exegetes and hermeneutists face similar challenges as other scholars in the translation of the *doul*-stem word. Like the Greek Bible translators, and not unlike Josephus and Philo, twentieth-century Igbo Bible translators face the challenge of translating the `ebed-pais-doulos* term in a way that retains the dignity of the word. Translators utilize two Igbo words *ohù* and *odibo* to translate the *doul*-stem word. While both words connote various degrees of slavery and servitude, they differ markedly in the concrete. In its common usage, *ohù* represents slave or slavery in

---

21. Lozano-Díaz, "Ignored Virgin or Unaware Women," 210.

the absolute; *odibo* stands for steward or one in temporary service of another.

The problem of translating *doulē* is evident in its rendering in the Igbo Catholic Bible as well as the Igbo Protestant Bible. The Igbo Catholic Bible displays some inconsistency in its rendering. For example, it renders the term handmaid, *doulē* when Hannah self-designates herself in 1 Samuel 1:11 as *ohù*. This same text also utilizes *ohù* to designate Hagar, the slave girls of Sara, in Genesis16: 1. But the Septuagint designates the handmaid Hannah, *doulē* in the Samuel text and Hagar *paidiskē* in the Genesis text. In the Book of Judith, the text renders *doulē, odibo*. More critically, the Catholic and the Protestant Igbo Bible translation of the *doulē* in Luke 1:38 differ significantly. While the Catholic Igbo Bible renders *doulē, odibo*, in this text, the Protestant Igbo Bible translates the word as *ohù*. Translations such as this can become problematic in Christian women's self-understanding, Catholics and Protestant alike, in Igbo society. Given the role of women in the African church, a redeemed interpretation of *doulē*, can enrich not only Christian communities but societies both in Igboland but in the Continent as a whole.

DOULAS FIGURES IN THE HEBREW BIBLE AND IN THE SEPTUAGINT

The Bible holds several examples of *doulas*, Israel's great women. These matriarchs distinguished themselves by their freedom for service to God in family and society at large. Because service to the community marks God's servants; service becomes the quintessential character of the *doulē*.

The arrays of Israel's *doulas* represent many unsung heroines of Scriptures. These include Ruth (Ruth 2:13), Hannah (1 Sam 1:11), Abigail (1 Sam 25:24), the Medium of Endor (1 Sam 28:21), the wise woman of Tekoah (2 Sam 14:6), Bathsheba (1 Kgs 1: 17), the Shunammite woman (2 Kgs 4: 8–37), Esther (Add Esth 14: 17–18), and Judith (Jdt 11:5, 16). Israel's *doulas* descended not from a monolithic stock. These represent women of different backgrounds, cultures, times, and genre with the status of being insiders, outsiders, captives, concubines, queens, widows, childless women, mothers, pagans, peacemakers, the wealthy, and priestesses. One thing these women have in common is their capacity for self-gift. This *"delicate and attentive service of others"*[22] symbolizes the *doulē*. Drawing from the examples of the narratives of Ruth, Abigail, Esther, and Judith, I show how these *doulas*, embodied service. Moreover, this narrative highlights the wisdom of the experience of these matriarchs, stories that can challenge modern day women to greater accomplishments.

Doulē Ruth

The narrative of the *doulē* Ruth in the Bible is located in the lands of Moab-Bethlehem. Citing the story of Ruth in Bethlehem makes it highly symbolic. Bethlehem (*beth* = house; *lehem* = bread), house of bread. Where bread denotes abundance, Bethlehem also means house of plenty. Bethlehem, house of plenty, rings with symbolic significance. Following from the etymology of the word, the significance of Jesus' birth in Bethlehem—house of plenty—lends support to the good news of abundant life that the Gospel portends (cf. John 10:10). By employing the imagery to locate the story, the author simultaneously provides the reader a window through which to view the indignity women suffer in the house of plenty, and how women can overcome structural injustice to become full participants in the community.

The narrative tells of two widows, Naomi and Ruth. Naomi, a native of Bethlehem and Ruth, a Moabite, return to Bethlehem from economic exile in the land of Moab. We thus establish that Ruth becomes a foreigner in the land of Israel. Moab was considered Israel's traditional enemy, and Ruth showed fortitude in venturing into enemy's territory. Ruth is also an "orphan." She is orphaned by choice. She turned away from her mother' house (Ruth 1:8) to follow her mother in-law, Naomi into another land. Ruth places herself under the care of the God of Israel, pleading with her mother-in-law "your people will be my people, and your God my God" (Ruth 1:16). Hence, Ruth, the widow, orphan, and the stranger, symbolized the truly poor according to biblical standard. Normally, this category of the poor has no connection whatsoever to patriarchal figures, that is, a father, husband or son

In a similar vein, Naomi also had no connection to patriarchy either. A widow deprived of husband Elimelech, and two sons Mahlon and Chilion, by death. Painfully aware of her social status, Naomi, whose

---

22. The Constitutions of the Handmaids of the Holy Child Jesus, article 12.

name means pleasant, took a new name, *Mara*, on arriving in her native Bethlehem. *Mara* is not without significance, a true irony, given that she was now in the house of plenty. Remarkably, the name, *Mara*, meaning bitter, symbolized the existential reality of a childless widow within her community of plenty. Ruth and Naomi remained marginal figures as well as poor in the community because of their non-connection to a patriarchal figure. Patriarchy is defined as the rule of the fathers. If non-attachment to patriarchy basically qualifies one as poor, by implication, a female human being qua female represents the poor *par excellence*—her sex already defines her. Thus, a "preferential option for the poor" of necessity takes women into consideration. In chapter four, I discuss the how certain seemingly innocuous female names automatically situate a girl-child in the category of the poor. Being marginal and poor, therefore, women lack full social participation. But being poor does not necessarily mean being poverty stricken. Neither does being poor suggest a lack of agency, as the story of Ruth obviously demonstrates. Furthermore, being poor may not denote powerlessness either. As Nigerian novelist and poet, Ben Okri strongly suggests, "There is no such thing as a powerless people."[23] Perhaps the liberative dimension of this tale makes it important to both Jews and Christians alike.

In the Jewish tradition, the Book of Ruth is part of Israel's wisdom tradition, one of the five books that make up the *Megilloth*, or "Scrolls," a special collection that includes Song of Songs, Ecclesiastes, Lamentations, and Esther. Curiously, Israel's wisdom-tradition often situates female characters squarely at the center of Jewish life. In Judaism, the story of Ruth is read every year during the Feast of *Shavuot* (Weeks), which Christians know as Pentecost. Ruth and Naomi, principal characters of the tale, represent *doulas* figures in ancient Israel. The story has been of special interest to Christians since Matthew lists Ruth among the ancestors of Jesus (Mt 1:5).

Some interpreters and commentators on the story, however, present this fascinating tale primarily from the prism of the objectification of women, particularly sexual exploitation. The keen sense of community, which the principal characters represent, escapes the attention of those exegetes. Reading from a wisdom tradition, the fullness of life, which emerges from a fuller sense of community rather than exploitation, represents the central argument of this narrative. The story's subtlety is

---

23. Okri, *A Way of Being Free*, 103.

seen in its brilliance, it introduces perhaps the furthermost of Israel's matriarchs and the ancestor of its prominent king, David. The Book of Ruth is perhaps the only one in the Old Testament that offers a wonderful example of a woman, who regardless of her ordinariness does great things in the name of the LORD. Both women further the covenant by engaging in day-to-day events, rather than grandiose or majestic projects. They were humans in their own rights. Moreover, the vividness and integrity of its main characters, which captures the audience, demonstrate covenant fidelity.

This multi-layered narrative captures succinctly the themes of covenant, community, solidarity, and human flourishing. Fundamentally, the story of Ruth represents a liberative event that can be appropriated, particularly by women who find themselves in the shadows of life.

In this tale, the narrator employs metaphors, drama, and innuendos to tell in a terse form a story of women in a situation of unredeemed patriarchal sexism. In providing only a few details in the narrative, the author allows readers to reach their own conclusions and learn their own lessons. The story of Ruth and Naomi represents a tale of fidelity and friendship. Theirs was a friendship between two women of dissimilar background, who stuck together to keep community alive. In this narrative the character of Ruth, whose name means friend when translated, is consistent with reclaiming and securing human dignity where it has been denied or constricted by dominant structures. The conclusions to the story of Ruth catapult her into the genealogy of Jesus Christ in the New Testament, reminding the reader of the impact of this seemingly inconsequential story. The narrative calls to mind an understanding of possibilities and beauty that the Okri notes: "It would seem a miraculous feat, but it is possible for the unvalued ones to help create a beautiful new era in human history. New vision should come from those who suffer most and who love life the most. This marvelous responsibility of the unheard and the unseen resides in this paradox."[24] Paradoxically, the story exposes the notion of power and powerlessness. It also points to where such resides in society. Most importantly the story provides a lens through which to view and evaluate covenantal relationship, which is the groundswell of social justice.

Membership in a covenantal relationship presupposes relationality as well as communicability. Out of the relationality and communicability

24. Okri, *Way of Being Free*, 103.

paradigm emerges the concept of social justice. The term social justice derives from two Hebrew words, *sedaqah* and *mispat*. American biblical scholar, John R. Donahue states that the "English versions, *sedaqah* [*sdq*] is translated 'righteousness' and *mispat* 'justice or judgment.'"[25] Donahue further articulates the social dimension of *sdq* and *mispat* thus, "Biblical justice is embedded in those very narratives that form a people's self-identity; actions that manifest concern for the weak and vulnerable become mandated in law and are not, as often thought today as supererogatory; and biblical justice always has a 'prophetic dimension,' by virtue of entering into conflict with oppressive structures of injustice."[26] Biblical justice awakes moral obligation for everyone, men and women alike. Moral commitments emerge from the community's common quest to grow into full humanity, to flourish together. Furthermore, social justice is part of the Deuteronomic idea of community. Ideally, in this community, no needy person exists. This means that the prophetic dimension of social justice challenges oppressive structures and calls upon the community to a greater sensitivity to the weak and vulnerable.

Spohn makes contemporaneous the Deuteronomic idea of justice thus, "Deuteronomy stresses the contemporary claim of the covenant on all subsequent generations and reinforces a hermeneutics of present memory."[27] Within the biblical justice tradition, dignity can become secured in an environment where solidarity informs relationships. In this sense, solidarity guarantees that no one is left out of the community's conversation, no voice is silenced, and no one is left in the shadow. Ruth and Naomi understood the implications of covenantal relationship and wasted no time in pursuing their rights. The handmaid Ruth and her mother in-law utilized the full extent of the *Law* to "liberate" themselves from the shadows to the light. They made their voices heard. Contrary to what is presumed in the culture of the period, the story reveals that Ruth and Naomi were not handmaids of men. The idea of the handmaid as that which accompanies in a subordinate manner did not fit into the category of these *doulas*. A cursory discussion on the *doulē* Abigail yields a similar understanding.

---

25. Donahue, "The Bible and Catholic Teaching: Will This Engagement Lead to Marriage," 14.

26. Donahue, "The Bible and Catholic Teaching," 15.

27. William, *What Are They Saying*, 60.

Doulē Abigail

The story of Abigail in the Bible is very brief and undeveloped. I consider this short story significant in the retrieval process of *doulas* characteristics from the Hebrew Scriptures. We first encounter Abigail in 1 Samuel Chapter 25. The Hebrew name "my father is joy" is suggestive of a wealthy parentage. She was married to a wealthy rancher from Maon named Nabal. Nabal owned a prosperous business in Carmel. But this wealthy businessman was described as wicked by one of his servants. We learn from his wife, Abigail, the full meaning of her husband's name when she beseeched David: "Let not my lord pay attention to that worthless man Nabal, for he is just like his name. Fool is his name, and he acts the fool" (I Sam 25:25). The narration writes in the significance of the name, Nabal, into his character and goes on to contrast Nabal's churlish and ill-mannered behavior with his wife's good nature.

Abigail, a kind and wise woman, self-designates herself, *doulē*. Her self-assertion as servant emerges from a profound sense of humility. Assuming a position of humility enabled her to engage with success the precarious life's situation occasioned by her imprudent husband. Nabal, a man of high socioeconomic status, could not discern the danger of confrontation with the servants of David, a warrior on the run. Nabal's wickedness and fool-hardiness differ sharply from Abigail's kindness, wisdom, and keen insights.

On learning of her husband's behavior toward David's men, without losing time, Abigail, a true *doulē*, single-handedly, engaged David, Israel's greatest warrior of the time. Where her husband was hostile to David's servant from his privileged position, Abigail, on the other hand, assumed a disadvantaged position. She went out to the "enemy's camp" to sue for peace. She rode through the roughest terrain, "through a mountain defile riding by an ass" (1 Sam 25:20), to fulfill her mission. As a typical *doulē*, she made the journey not without gifts. Abigail loaded up her donkey with provision for David and his men. For the one single purpose of defending life, the life of her husband Nabal and that of the whole family, this woman of high status humbles herself before an outlaw on the run. She acts towards David and addresses him as though he is the lord and she the servant "My lord, let the blame be mine." Abigail takes the blame of Nabal's miscalculated ignorance. As Adele Berlin puts it, "Abigail's good manner and diplomatic strategy succeed in protecting

Nabal from David's wrath."[28] By her humble gesture, she demonstrates that service and humility cannot be separated. Service and humility exemplified by this *doulē* represents that which Jesus would later enact in the washing of his disciples' feet (John 13:1–17); foot-washing thus, becomes an allegory of humility. William Spohn describes the foot-washing in the gospel of John thus: "humble service, equality, concrete compassion, voluntary relinquishment."[29]

Indeed, when David asked for Abigail's hand in marriage, she responds "Behold, your handmaid is a servant to wash the feet of the servants of my lord" (1 Sam 25:41). In the end, the compassion that Nabal could not offer David and his men, the *doulē* Abigail accomplished. Although her peace initiative was fraught with impossibilities, she succeeded. God made the impossible possible for this *doulē* who dared to act.

The profound faith of this heroine moved her to prophecy. As a true worshipper of God, Abigail perceived the potentials in David. Her prophetic word foreshadows David's future kingship. At the death of her husband, Nabal, Abigail became David's wife. Abigail's subsequent marriage to David makes sense when read from the context of conflict and hardship. Under normal circumstances, such a marriage may perhaps not be possible. But the marriage represents the bind in which many women find themselves in extremely harsh and life threatening situations. The character of the biblical Esther emerges also from a similar life and death circumstance.

Doulē Esther

The author of the book of Esther provides genealogy for his main character. Esther was the daughter of Aminadab, cousin and adopted daughter of Mordecai, who was forced by circumstances to become the queen of King Ahasuerus (485—465 B.C.) The story of Esther represents a more complex scenario than that of Abigail. While the Abigail story was about a single household, that of Esther was about an entire group of people, the Diaspora Jews in Babylon. There are two versions to the Book of Esther, the Hebrew Esther written about the 4th century, B.C., and the Greek version (Septuagint, LXX) of the Hebrew Bible Book of Esther written about the second or first century, B.C. Our concern in

---

28. Berlin, "Abigail," 43–44.
29. Spohn, *Go and Do Likewise*, 62.

this narrative, however, is the role this female character played in offering new hope to a burdened people. I, therefore, draw insights from both versions of the Book to offer an understanding of role of this *doulē* character in the context of a people struggling for survival.

Like Abigail, Esther showed intelligence and wisdom in navigating the difficult and hostile environment of her station. This young Jewish maiden engaged her context from her deep faith in the God of her ancestors in the face of imminent death. She approached God as God's *doulē*, "*he doule sou*" (Add Esth 14:17, 18), a slave. Addressing oneself as slave before a superior power articulates distance and dependence.

The idea of distance and dependence resonates in the prayer Esther offers in preparation to appear before the King. (Add Esth "C" 14–30).

> Esther's prayer "identifies her as fundamentally a relational self, although the self's relationality is not dependent on the immediate presence of any human community or individual." By making herself "fully transparent before an Other whom she addresses directly and incessantly," Esther puts herself into a personal and intimate relationship with God. This God, Esther's personal confidant, is not the detached transcendent "First Mover" of Aristotle. God, even in silence, is immanent and maintains somewhat permeable boundaries. At the same time, the relationship is by no means equal. It is one of utter and complete subservience to God, like an ideal subject to a king.[30]

The degree of commitment and dependency on God expressed by the *doulē* Esther fosters personal transformation. In this case, her transformation translates into totally engaging her world within the context of community.

Fundamentally, Esther's complete subservience to God derives from her complete faith in the supernatural power. The authors of *Religion and the Self in Antiquity* showed that Esther's faith experience grounds her courage to take risks on behalf of the community.[31] A combination of faith, wit and talent enabled this young *doulē* to reimagine an alternative scenario amidst the impending destruction that looms over her people. In the ancient Near East, it is often considered dangerous to approach the throne of a King without being summoned. Daring to come into the King's presence could lead to death. It is instructive that the

---

30. Brakke et al., "Introduction," 9.
31. Brakke et al.

warning did not stop Esther. She would go against the law if that would mean redemption for a doomed people. She realized that her privileges as queen were not just for her pleasure, but for service, particularly, to serve those at the margins, those without hope. In the face of imminent death, Esther showed sublime courage. This young *doulē* sums up her activism in these words, "I will go to the king, contrary to the law. If I perish, I perish!" (Esth. 4:16). Esther's utterance "If I perish, I perish" does not represent a fatalistic attitude. Rather, the position she took came out of one who had full trust in the LORD whose *doulē* she had become. Trusting in the LORD, she was prepared to face even death with confidence.

There is a way in which Esther's determination echoes the prophet Isaiah's self-offering "Here am I; send me!" (Isa 6:8), and Mary of Nazareth's *fiat* in Luke 1:38. This remarkable response can only come from one who has, and understands, the value of human dignity. Her ability to accept and negotiate ambiguous situations marks her as an excellent leader and servant of the people. Thus Esther became a savior figure for her generation. Not unlike other Israel's `ebed/doulos* figures, this Jewish *doulē* also imagines herself as a humble subject of the divine king. Esther Menn summed up the *doulē* Esther's position thus, "Esther . . . emphasizes her self-understanding primarily as a humble subject of the divine king by twice identifying herself as the deity's female slave ("your slave," *he doulē sou*, LXX Esth 14:17, 18). This repeated identification emphasizes that Esther owes her primary allegiance to God and not to the many others who claim her devotion and obedience within the layered hierarchical structures of her world."[32] Although the presentation of the *doulē* may be understood as subordinate within the multiple hierarchical relationships in which she functions; she, nonetheless, does not fit into the general patriarchal belief in female inferiority, dependence, and helplessness.[33] *Doulē* Esther's loyalty is primarily to God, not to the king.

Contrary to the patriarchal interpretation and claim of women's subordination, Israel's *doulas*, such as Esther, claimed full humanity with full voice and agency. As evident in the story, the voice of the subject was self-defining, liberative, and energizing. Voice proclaims a person as a conscious being capable of independent thought and action. Voice

---

32. Menn, "Prayer of the Queen: Esther's Religious Self in the Septuagint," 76.

33. Uzukwu, *Listening Church*, 141. See, also Schaberg, "Luke," 372.

ushers in a sense of new freedom, freedom for self-gift, meaning liberty to service.

The liberty to serve ranks high in the recovery of dignity. In the hierarchy of joy, Nigerian novelist and poet, Ben Okri places freedom next to the greatest joy of all, love.[34] Okri, however, stresses that freedom does not represent the goal of striving; freedom represents the beginning of the greatest possibilities of the human genius. The genius lies in the self-designated nature of freedom, "here I am," that is one's ability to make a self-gift of the self. *Doulē* Esther though in bodily captivity, had the inner freedom to make this gift. Dignity represents this freedom as the tortoise story in Chapter 4 amply suggests. Like some other *doulas* characters in the Hebrew Scriptures, who come into their own after men, create crises they cannot resolve themselves, Esther does rise to the occasion. She showed intelligence and wisdom in navigating the difficult and hostile environment of her station. This young Jewish maiden engaged her context from her deep faith in the God of her ancestors. Esther's position was not very different from that of *doulē* Judith whose act of self-gift saved her nation from annihilation.

Doulē Judith

> Now therefore, brethren, let us set an example to our brothers,
> for their lives depend upon us, and the sanctuary and the temple
> and the altar rest upon us (Jdt 8:24).

The Book of Judith is found in the deuterocanonical literature canonized in the Roman Catholic Bible. The name Judith means Judean woman or feminine of Judah. This literature about the Judeans provides a primary example of the distinguished service of the *doulē* in a Jewish society. Written about the second or early first century before the birth of Christ, this book that entertains as much as it defies, challenges Israel's covenant fidelity and suggests women's role in promoting and sustaining the covenant. Judith, a female character personifies that fidelity to which God summons the people.

Judith, a devout, affluent, and wise widow rescues her town from destruction. A woman of prayer and of action, she saves her people of Bethulia from the evil forces of the Assyrians that threaten to annihilate them. Not unlike Joshua, a *doulos kyriou*, this *doulē* offers her life for her

---

34. Okri, 126.

people. Accompanied by her faith in the God of Israel and her maidservant, Judith attempts the impossible. She invades an enemy camp. Like Moses, Judith stood as a bridge between God and her town's people (cf. Exod 32:32). Judith assumes leadership in order to avert the crisis that befell her people. Although in an extreme situation, Judith makes use of extreme means, in her prayer and song she questions military power and violence. A song, filled with appellations, by the people of Bethulia honored Judith's devotion, service, and valor. Judith's tenacity in fostering communal harmony legitimates the *doulē* claim of servant and leader.

A law-abiding woman, Judith sets an example for women by her bold faith. Her faith consists not only in beliefs but also in action and trust, which the people of Bethulia hailed. Her triumphant procession after the defeat of the Assyrian army is reminiscent of that of the Song of Miriam (Exod 15:1–16). This *doulē* figure was unconventional in her day in her military actions and in dealing with the male members of her society. Judith represents a type of womanhood whom the "favored" maiden from Nazareth typifies. The character of Judith was not lost on the Roman Catholic tradition in illuminating the character of Mary of Nazareth.

Roman Catholic piety in some way employs the character of Judith to characterize the Virgin Mary. Catholic worship and piety appropriate the song and appellations of Judith in the Liturgy of the Hours that celebrate the Virgin Mary. The Office of the Blessed Virgin Mary is replete with antiphons drawn from passages in the Book of Judith. Nowhere is the comparison of Mary and Judith more expressed than in a song composed by a French Roman Catholic priest, Spiritan Father Lucien Deiss. Deiss follows a long tradition of accommodating characteristics of Old Testament heroines to Mary in a song titled: "You are the honor; you are the glory of our people, Holy Virgin Mary,"[35] based on Judith 15:9–10.

Long before the song by Deiss, the image of Judith is immortalized in Roman Catholic iconography. Carefully scripted in a painting at the ceiling of the Sistine Chapel, one of the paintings represents Judith holding the severed head of Holofernes. Michelangelo presented three other Israelite models, pointing to Jesus as savior: Moses (bronze serpent), David (Goliath), and Esther (Haman on the gibbet). These four paintings represent four moments of salvation/deliverance in Israel's history. Note that two men and two women represent this sweep of Israel's history.

35. Deiss, *Biblical Hymns and Psalms*, 60–61.

The artist portrays the interdependence of women and men in combating forces that impinge on human dignity. These paintings, in a way, give credence to the redemptive role of Israel's *doulas* in salvation. In a very symbolic manner, these four paintings depicting moments in salvation history represent the equal value of men and women in on-going history. Amidst what scholars term a staunchly patriarchal culture, Israel's *doulas* served God and community with complete devotion. They function as neither appendage nor auxiliary to the male. By inscribing the images of the "savior" figures on the ceiling of the Sistine Chapel, the Catholic tradition makes an unequivocal statement on women's equal participation in church life. Indeed, the ethos of the Chapel demands retrieval and an interpretation in women's quest for a voice in church life.

The examples of Israel's *doulas* characters discussed in these pages bear "glad tidings" for contemporary women (Isa 41:27). They bring the Good News that God liberates the voiceless and the invisible, those at the margins of the dominant arena. In sum, this conscious designation of oneself as *doulē* articulates women's self-understanding as active participants in current processes. The self-assertion as *doulē* among these biblical characters contradicts claims that women in ancient Israel were nearly always victims of male dominance and seldom leaders or contributors to culture. It is particularly significant that the Roman Catholic celebrates the *doulē* tradition in worship and in song. For if these actions and words permeate the Roman Catholic traditions, why does the Church still keep women, the Catholic *doulas*, out of full participation in church life? A similar question can also be asked of society. Perhaps the various ways in which the dominant group continues to exclude the contemporary *doulas* from full participation in social processes accounts for the less than optimal realization of the synergy of human potential in contemporary society

3

The Handmaid: Mary of Nazareth

Introduction

WHO IS MARY OF Nazareth? Christian tradition characterizes Mary of Nazareth among others as a virgin, handmaiden, spouse, or mother. Scholars and commentaries, however, tend to ignore Mary's self-understanding in her assertion as *doulē kyriou* in Luke 1:38. Significantly, Mary's assertion as *doulē kyriou* directs our attention and imagination to discover who she truly is, and whom she serves as a handmaid. An exploration of this Lukan passage, Luke 1:26–38 reveals the profound qualities, ignored by interpreters that this Jewish woman possesses. Retrieving these characteristics provides an understanding to the character of Mary of Nazareth. On this basis, the use of the biblical passage becomes crucial in reassessing women's role in the African church and in society at large. In this chapter, I first recall the *doulē* tradition and the issue of identity. Then I offer a brief survey of the historical background of the Annunciation, and then proceed to retell from a new perspective what transpired between Mary and God's emissary, the angel Gabriel. I conclude with the outcome of Mary's divine encounter and how that can become a paradigm of universality for service and leadership. The retelling bears much on my experience as an African vowed religious. Most importantly, it derives from my experience as member of a religious community, Handmaids of the Holy Child Jesus, whose name derives from the Annunciation passage.

Doulē Tradition

The purpose of the Gospel is connected deeply with fostering abundant life (John 10:10). Striving for a bounteous life falls short, however, when a literal reading of Scripture hardens readers' imagination and creates blindness. Because the eternal quality of things or people is truer than its visible forms, literal readings of texts fall short of the Good News. That is to say, it empties the Gospel of its meaning – Immanuel, God-with-us. This becomes evident in the works done by some exegetes writing on the Annunciation narrative. These scholars, for example, move quickly through the passage to Mary's role as mother as though that was the only purpose of the passage. Like other parts of Scripture, depending on the community of interpreters, this Lukan passage can have a variety of meanings. I join my voice to others to suggest that this Lukan story is primarily about Mary of Nazareth and God's accomplishment.

Scholars who stress Mary's motherhood tend to ignore the very humble beginnings of God's creativity. The choice of Nazareth reflects such modest origins. God's choice of Nazareth, a town to which no Old Testament expectation was attached, represents a sign of the total newness of what God does. That is to say, God does not maintain *status quo*. The context of obscurity and insignificance enriches the narrative. In a place where according to Nathanael, "Can anything good come from Nazareth?" Luke invites the reader to experience greater things, new things important enough to involve an angelic messenger. Hence, this recognition of total newness out of humble origins gives impetus to the redemptive story of the teenage Jewish maiden from Nazareth.

Redemptive reading constitutes what Thomas R. Kopfensteiner called the *pharmakon*, that is to say, the remedy, or else, a way of rescuing the message of a text from the distance of culture, and what was foreign, is brought near. This new closeness is a proximity that "suppresses and preserves the cultural distance and includes the otherness with the ownness."[1] Within the tradition, there is an opportunity to take on new perspectives of thought and action. The significance in this case is that through a reading or an act of interpretation, the truth of the passage may be claimed continually and progressively by moral reasoning. Kopfensteiner says that reading is dynamic, and interpretation changes dynamically as the reader develops. In this way, biblical passages renew the self-understanding of the individual as well as the community, and can truly become redemptive.

---

1. Kopfensteiner, "Globalization and the Autonomy of Moral Reasoning: An Essay in Fundamental Moral Theology," 503.

The idea of redemption challenges one to redream and to reclaim one's place in the world. Redreaming and reclaiming one's place in the world involves a keen sense of imagination and a sustained act of maturation.[2] Besides, the challenge of self-becoming does not go without breaching and confounding the accepted frontiers according to the prophecy of Jeremiah. Jeremiah 1:10 proclaims: "See, I place my words in your mouth! This day I set you over nations and over kingdoms, to root up and to tear down, to destroy and to demolish, to build and to plant (Jer 1:10)." Jeremiah's prophecy challenges us to redream and to build a new world. But first, we must unearth and destroy the myths and realities, the misinterpretation, misrepresentation, and misappropriation of teachings of the old world that some have used to subordinate and marginalize other human beings. For this reason, it becomes important to evaluate critically the enduring interpretation of the Handmaid, so intricately woven into the tapestry of Roman Catholic religious imagination, and reassess its significance in fostering the abundant life.

The redemptive significance of the Lukan passage lies in its potential to further the Good News, bringing glad tidings to the poor, liberty to captives, vision to the blind, and release for the subjugated (Luke 4:17–18). A rereading of the narrative presents an avenue through which to access Mary's self-understanding. It provides a glimpse into Mary's experience of God in her cultural context. Pondering on and probing further the passage brings to light the energy that made her proclaim herself, *doulē kyriou*, the slave of the LORD. In so doing, this new understanding announces liberty, visibility and vocality for the disenfranchised. In addition, the renewed meaning of the Handmaid in the sense of *doulē kyriou* reestablishes Mary as a model of positive self-identification for Christians, women and men whose baptism fundamentally makes them servants of each other.

Establishing Identity

Whose Handmaid? To whom does Mary belong? Establishing the identity of Mary is central to the issue of women's advancement, since many Christian women appropriate her as a role model. The question of identity refers to the conscious dimension of character, the deliberate core of personal experience, which according to William Spohn is

---

2. Okri, *Way of Being Free*, 55.

shaped by our most basic commitments and convictions. Spohn goes on to state that identity names that which stays the same in the stream of consciousness, the continuity to a personal history.[3] Identity represents the basic sense of who we are and the horizon of our uniqueness. Since identity is best captured by looking at our most important relationships, Mary's relationships with Joseph, the angel Gabriel, Elizabeth, and John the Baptist, the characters in the passage under review provide the window into whose handmaid she truly is. Through these interactions personal continuity is determined by the persons and causes to which one has committed oneself, and the persons who have promised themselves to us. Thus, identity comes from identification with specific people and causes. Mary's sense of identity was radically changed when she encountered the angel, "Hail O highly favored one" (v. 28). Her response to the situation truly defined her. In this regard, a close reading of the Lukan passage, 1:26–28, offers the opportunity to engage the story.

The close reading process I have chosen derives from the insight of Old Testament exegete, Walter Brueggemann. Brueggemann categorized the three-step close reading as utilizing the force of imagination, hosting of intertextuality, and pondering of ideology.[4] I have chosen the exegetical technique of Brueggeman because this technique resonates with the Igbo way and manner of storytelling. Different strands from narrative are woven together according to a set pattern, producing a fresh contemporaneous story. At this juncture, having the Lukan text (Luke 1:26–38) on hand makes reading easily accessible.

The Text: Luke 1:26–38

v. 26 In the sixth month, the angel Gabriel was sent from God to a town of Galilee called Nazareth,

v. 27 to a virgin betrothed to a man named Joseph, of the house of David, and the virgin's name was Mary.

v. 28 And coming to her, he said, "Hail, favored one! The Lord is with you."

v. 29 But she was greatly troubled at what was said and pondered what sort of greeting this might be.

v. 30 Then the angel said to her, "Do not be afraid, Mary, for you have found favor with God.

v. 31 Behold, you will conceive in your womb and bear a son, and you shall name him Jesus.

3. Spohn, *Go and do Likewise*, 24.
4. Brueggemann, *Word Militant*, 75–82.

v. 32 He will be great and will be called Son of the Most High, and the Lord God will give him the throne of David his father,

v. 33 and he will rule over the house of Jacob forever, and of his kingdom there will be end."

v. 34 But Mary said to the angel, "How can this be, since I have no relations with a man?"

v. 35 And the angel said to her in reply, "The holy Spirit will come upon you, and the power of the Most High will overshadow you. Therefore the child to be born will be called holy, the Son of God.

v. 36 And behold, Elizabeth, your relative, has also conceived a son in her old age, and this is the sixth month for her who was called barren;

v. 37 for nothing will be impossible for God."

v. 38 Mary said, "Behold, I am the handmaid of the Lord, May it be done to me according to your word." Then the angel departed from her.

Historical Background

The New Testament Books of the Gospel of Luke and the Acts of the Apostles are two complementary volumes by the same author. The infancy story of Luke 1–2, for example, corresponds to the infancy of the Church (Acts 1–2). Mary plays a significant role in both instances. Their structures complement each other in many ways. The author situates the story of the Mary of Nazareth in first century Palestine. Politically, Palestine came under Roman control, first partially in 63 before the birth of Christ and fully in A.D. 6. Jesus was born when Caesar Augustus was Emperor. Pontius Pilate was the agent of Emperor Tiberias and the Roman governor under whom Jesus died.

Political repression under Roman rule heightened Israel's expectation of a messiah who would rescue them from the oppressive Roman rule. Mary of Nazareth was no stranger to these events. She was not separated from her people's experience. As a Jewess, she participated and shared the messianic hope of her people, a mark of Israel's religious identity drawn primarily from the Temple and the Torah. This identity embodies the history of Israel's covenant, the story of salvation. In writing the Annunciation narrative, therefore, the author seeks to make contemporaneous this salvation story for his gentile audience.

Written in Greek about 80 A. D., the Gospel according to Luke does not claim to be an eyewitness account. Rather, the author declared himself to be handing down a received tradition from eyewitnesses. He maintained that his narrative was to enlighten his new converts.

Luke's assertion represents the Gospel as an interpretative act of social reconstruction in the face of a new social reality. This story focuses on the character of the central figure in Luke 1:26–38, Mary, the Nazareth maiden. In seeking to gain a different kind of insight from this narrative I have forgone discussion of Mary's virginity or motherhood. Christology is also neglected in favor of the close focus on the self-understanding Mary evidences in her proclamation of *doulē kyriou*. The author of Luke-Acts presents the narrative in the form of drama and dialogue. Gabriel, the emissary of God, and Mary, a maiden from Nazareth, represent the main characters. The storyline is about the birth of the Son of God, Jesus, whom Mary would bear as well as name.

Unraveling the metaphor of the *doulē* in Luke 1:26–38 goes beyond examining the historical contemporary context. It requires reading many versions of the same story; across certain time periods. In the previous chapter, I rendered the *doulē* narrative from deep within the Jewish Scriptures. In a world where more than one text exists, that is, a world of plurality, a given text may describe, but if another text intrudes, it is possible for that text to redescribe reality.[5] A close reading of Luke 1:26–38 attempts to redescribe the maiden from Nazareth by drawing insights from other texts.

CLOSE READING OF LUKE 1:26–38

Rhetorical Analysis

A close reading of Luke 1:26–38 reveals that Mary was an active participant in this Lukan story. Although Scripture provides slender details of Mary's social position, a synchronic and diachronic reading of the Gospel gives a slight clue about Mary's sociocultural context. For sure, she was what we may call a small town girl, unsophisticated in many ways, yet profoundly knowledgeable in others. But this small town maiden was about to enter into the majestic presence of God. In a characteristic Hebraic sense, where God's messenger is present, there God is. Here, Gabriel represents God in this event that began to unfold in the backwater Galilean town, Nazareth. It is typical of Luke that Nazareth, as a place which is of no particular interest, where we find the absentees of history, should light up with marvelous significance. Emmaus

---

5. Brueggemann, *Word Militant*, 23.

would also feature likewise at the end of Luke's Gospel (24:13–35). The unimaginable was occurring; God came to a rural community to speak with a young unmarried female. The author, however, wasted no time in confronting the reader with the fact that this young female is bound to a system that is patriarchal.

The author first presents Mary in direct relationship to a male figure, Joseph, her betrothed. It appears that according to the culture of the time, this female character could not stand on her own personal recognition. The context suggests that Mary receives her identification as a person from her familial relationship to a man. The female's relevance depends on this relationship. Feminist scholar Ivoni Richter Reimer describes the setting in the context of first century Palestine, "In the Greco-Roman and Jewish society in the first century . . . Judaism emphasized that both men and women were made in the image of God, thus establishing equality between the sexes. But practically, and in daily life, a woman was for the most part only valued when she lived in a condition of patriarchal dependency on a man, either her father or her husband."[6] Although Mary and Gabriel represent the principal characters in this drama, the narrator presents Joseph to the reader before Mary. Introducing Mary after Joseph emphasizes female dependence on the male for legitimacy. Thus, in first phase of her appearance, the author subtly renders the young maiden partially invisible, seen only through the lens of a male relative, Joseph. By introducing patriarchal structure at the beginning of the call narrative, Luke sets the stage for the reversal that the Galilean maiden portends.

Within the dominant structure, Mary not only is invisible, she also remains voiceless. This voiceless and penumbra shadow existence, however, would undergo transformation by the power of the One who makes all things new. Transformation came to Mary gradually. In verse 28, Mary advances from the shadows of patriarchal enclave and from a position of non-participation to begin her pilgrimage. British anthropologist, Victor Turner, describes liminality as the state and process of mid-transition in a rite of passage.[7] The verses that follow represent Mary's *liminal* period, a period fraught with ambiguity. During this stage, Mary passes through a cultural realm that has few or none of the attributes of the past or coming state, the most significant; being that

---

6. Reimer, "Life Calls for Triumph and Celebration," 90.

7. Turner, *Image and Pilgrimage*, 249–250.

The Handmaid: Mary of Nazareth 45

she would have a child out of wedlock. Liminality for Mary represents a time when the old configurations of social reality increasingly appear to be in jeopardy. It represents for her a time of uncertainty, yet she must participate in the process. Mary's liminal stage is reminiscent of that of Moses, Israel's great liberator (Exod 33:17). Mary's call in Luke Chapter one, has a certain pattern to it that fits the call of great prophets and leaders in the Bible. As with Moses, for example, God first appears to Mary (v. 26–27) and explains the reason for the visit (v. 28). Next God commissions her to a task (v. 31–33). Mary objects (v. 34) but God reassures her and insists (v. 35). Finally, God follows with a prediction (v. 36–37). And Mary accepts (v. 38).

Like Moses, who steps out of cultural norms to a new vocation of leadership, Mary's vocation would consist in a "leading out," and in engendering a new people. Entering into communion with the people would form part of her new mission. Elizabeth echoes the communion in beatitudes (Luke 1: 42) similar to those of Uzziah saluting Judith, "Blessed are you, by the Most High God, above all the women on earth" (Jdt 13:17). With Mary stepping out from the shadows towards the light, an alternative process begins.

New alternatives began to emerge for this Nazareth maiden. First she receives a new identity and a new name: "favored one."[8] In the greeting, "Hail, favored one," a divine presence sounds in the context of a hitherto known absence, the absentee of history. Favored one, Mary's new name, represents a term of endearment and the embodiment of her new role. With a new identity, Mary begins a journey towards newness. From this unique position, the story becomes hers.

Mary does not remain stoic in the face of the heavenly greeting. She responds, though not with words. Mary responds meditatively with fright. Fear represents a legitimate response of a self-conscious awareness. Perhaps if she could speak, she would have said "Who am I to be so highly favored!" No doubt, the upbringing of this Jewish maiden may have prepared and enabled her to sense the freight of the divine salutation, "favored one!" The divine messenger deigned to console the frightened maiden, "fear not," the angel reassures her. The words "fear not," means that God, the one who liberates, has overridden and nullified all the powers of fear. Fear for this young maiden became the awe that disposes her to obedience to the call the angel offers. Spohn puts

---

8. Fitzmyer, *Gospel According to Luke*, 345.

it this way, "Fear of the Lord" does not paralyze; it becomes awe that disposes to obedience to the call. In a word, the encounter becomes "dispositional representation," a scenario for action that is engraved in the heart's basic tendencies."[9] The words "fear not," therefore, cancel the fears fostered by the socio-cultural structures that held Mary back in the shadows of history. The assurance heralds a radically new beginning for Joseph's betrothed.

Fear not, represents not only a word of consolation but also a word that jars. Brueggemann named this scenario "comfort-with-disturbance."[10] Comfort-with-disturbance requires Mary to come to terms with the strange new world that the angel offers. That strange new world represents the "alternative" domain of the incarnate God, the world where the female fears not, the *uwa-t-uwa*, a world within a world within a world . . . I describe in chapter 4. In this alternative world, there is no restriction on the female imagination, on her ability to deal with life as a whole. Mary would conceive, bear a God-son and name him. Strangely, the maiden receives the power of naming; she names a male, her own son. To name a child was no ordinary function in Mary's Jewish society. In this society, power resides in the one who names. To name a person represents a momentous task. To name a person implies knowledge of the one named, the reason being that names metaphorically represent the essence of a person. Although Mary did not choose the name of her son, she of all humans was privy to the significance of the name. Listening to the angel, she knew, pondered, and treasured the contradiction that was to become part of her life.

In verse 34, the author subtly presents a young woman with a capacity to see and to face contradictions. She had the ability to analyze, to question, and ultimately to make a decision. This young woman, who, having weighed the angel's greetings and recognized the complexity of the angel's mission, speaks out! For the first time in the synoptic Gospels, the reader hears a female voice, the utterance of Mary of Nazareth. She asks the messenger, "How can this be, since I have no relations with a man?"

---

9. Spohn, *Go and Do Likewise*, 130.
10. Brueggemann, *Word Militant*, 9.

Mary Speaks: First Voice in the Synoptic Gospels

Mary's question is profoundly significant. The inquiry represents a significant element in discovering Mary's self-understanding. That Mary actually asked a question represents a ground-breaking event. There is no minimizing the subject of the question, "How can this be, since I have no relations with a man?" But the critical issue is the fact that Mary actually questions an authority figure. Mary's power to question contradicts assertions of some feminist/womanist theologians who claim that the Virgin Mary cannot be a model of a liberated human being.[11] Because these theologians could not access Mary's voice, they project her as mute, invisible, and a mere object acted upon. For them, this aspect of the narrative or rather voice is not sufficiently abstract. Carol Myers puts it this way: "feminist scholars find it difficult to let go of the notion that 'the more abstract and transcendent something is, the better it is.'"[12] Myers further states that "such attitudes must be recognized as culture-bound constructions of Western religious studies and not a reflection of the 'lived' reality of other peoples, or even of people today, as those studying 'religion on the ground' in America are discovering."[13] In not recognizing Mary's daring to speak, these feminists/womanists scholars make her a powerless woman.

But evidence in the passage suggests otherwise. Mary's question also contradicts interpretations that cast her in the role of a human slave. Slaves in her day were "mute" before authority figures. In that day, female slaves had no voice concerning engendering offspring for her owner.[14] Can a human slave/*doulos* question a superior in first century Palestine? Does the slave seek knowledge apart from the master's orders? A slave is legally incapable of entering into a new bond, but Mary did enter into a new bond, meaning that she was not a slave in the sense of the New Testament use of the *doul*-stem word. Contextually, in Palestine of that day, the role Mary played in the Incarnation is not consistent with that of a *paidiskē*, a servile. Her character remains consonant with that of Israel's *doulas*. These women were community leaders. The literary de-

---

11. Williams, *Sisters in the Wilderness*, 182.
12. Myers, *Households and Holiness*, 61.
13. Myers, *Households and Holiness*.
14. Glancy, *Slavery in Early Christianity*, 17.

vice of interspersing Mary's narrative with the story of the birth of John the Baptist serves to introduce John as a precursor to Jesus.

John's role in the narrative provides first-hand evidence of Mary's free social status, which her voice confirms. The modest maiden fears not, she musters courage, and questions the heavenly visitor, "how can it be, since I have no relations with a man?" The maiden questions because she seeks to become a full participant in the unfolding God-act.

Mary's first voice in the synoptic Gospels largely goes uncelebrated. These first words draw little attention from exegetes of both sexes. Female as well as male exegetes tend to underrate or rather ignore this first instance of a female voice recorded in the Synoptic Gospel. Very often exegetes move quickly from verse 33 to 38 ignoring the groundbreaking verse 34. Regrettably, the active participation of the *doulē* in this Luke passage tends to escape the attention and imagination of women scholars as well. Beverly Roberts Gaventa, for example, in her entry on "Mary" in *Eerdmans Dictionary of the Bible* moves from verse 33 to verse 38 with no word on verse 34. She stated, "When the angel Gabriel announces to this unmarried young woman that she is to bear a child, she responds with the consent of a disciple, "Here am I, the servant of the Lord . . ." (Luke 1:38a)."[15] Evidence in the text demonstrates that Mary did not respond quickly. When the angel delivered the message, Mary's first action was to question. She seeks understanding. Only after receiving clarifications from the angel Gabriel, did she make her decision. Thus by asking question, and reflecting on the clarifications, she could make an informed decision, knowing full well she was risking her life. She knows she was stepping out beyond her social scope in talking with the angel. The angel's commission to her puts her at risk of being stoned to death. She questions because she knows she is stepping further out of bounds. Humanly speaking, we never really know beforehand the full implications of the choices we make. This perhaps is the mystery of life. The grace of God enables us to live as events unfold; hence the appropriateness of the greeting "full of grace," as Elizabeth would later salute Mary.

Moving quickly through the story and paying little attention to verse 34 is but a literal reading of the story. Such reading leaves untapped the potential for growth and positive self-identification, inherent in the narrative. Curiously, a fuller meaning of Mary's *fiat*, in verse 38 depends

---

15. Gaventa, "Mary," 864.

on a critical reading of verse 34. Mary's *fiat* must be understood in the context of her question, "How can this be?" Mary's question is *prima facie* evidence that she is an active participant in the divine drama to which she agreed to become a participant. Her voice celebrates the fact that she is a subject who had voice and agency. This image of the maiden from Nazareth deconstructs the age-worn idea of her silence and utter submissiveness. The informative-performative event of verse 34 represents a "voice from below." Such voice from below defies silencing.

The "voice from below" represents the truth concerning the identity of Mary of Nazareth. Thus the voice makes her visible and testifies to the dignity she possesses. Movement towards visibility comes from daring to speak. This movement coming from below can be seen in some Psalms in the Hebrew Bible. The voice from below refusing the silence, speaking the truth amid power, speaking truth to holiness and evoking newness, that voice according to Brueggeman can be seen in the richness of complaint psalms and lament psalms and psalms of rage and hate and resentment.[16] In this case, speech creates possibilities.

This possibility transforms and transports Mary from the shadows to the light. She moves progressively from a system that held her bound to another human person to becoming a free person who can speak her mind. Mary's encounter with the divine gradually reverses the status quo reshaping her identity from patriarchal "servitude" to service of the living God. Her question makes her privy to her master's dealings (Matt 10:25). Indeed, she was not simply a servant, but a friend of God (John 15:15), because the LORD has taken her completely into confidence. Thus, in daring to speak out, to question the divine messenger, Mary enters in God's confidence.

Readings that circumvent the active voice of Mary continue to reinforce and celebrate women's silence and invisibility in social processes. Verse 34 challenges that silence. Does not the reverberating of the female voice in the Incarnation narrative challenge women's silencing and subordination both in society and church life? In speaking, Mary insists that silence even in the presence of the divine cannot authenticate the *status quo*. By breaking the silence, she redescribes her world. The very act of voicing lifted her higher than the conditions and possibilities of the world she inhabited.

---

16. Brueggemann, *Word Militant*, 154.

Women, particularly African women cannot underestimate the potential for positive growth inherent in this singular voice of the Nazareth maiden. Since a female voice questions the patriarchal social structure and in the process demystifies traditional images of the "handmaid," Mary's first recorded words escape the attention of the dominant interpretation of this passage. On the contrary, most teaching and preaching on this passage selectively have upheld those sections of submission to proscribe women's freedom. In the end, the disproportional emphasis placed on Mary's *fiat* in verse 38a, obliterates the ground breaking verse 34. Most importantly, the fact that a shadowy female figure from obscure Nazareth could question an authority confounds dominant interpretation.

Mary's daring response elicited a revelation. Her inquisitiveness brought the story to a high point, the introduction of the Holy Spirit. Mary's question invites the Holy Spirit into the scene, not just the Holy Spirit in isolation but the Trinitarian dimension of the Incarnation, "Let us make..." (Gen 1:26). God the Father, through the emissary Gabriel, while speaking of the Son, introduces the Holy Spirit. The Trinitarian community converges to create. In their relationality bonded in a mutual outpouring of love, they bring about newness, affirming that creativity takes place within a community. Not totally exclusive in their relationship, the Trinity makes a place for humanity, the viewer. As Richard Gula puts it, "the viewer feels invited to sit at the table with three persons to share in the divine community."[17] Thus the Word became flesh in community of God and human, a female, Mary of Nazareth representing humanity. Luke shows in the passage that the Word became human, not in ignorance or by coercion, but in full participation and consent of all the actors, God and humankind. Subsequent events in Mary's life reveal the possibility of a new world the Holy Spirit makes possible. Luke artfully employs contrast to demonstrate God's possibilities and newness.

Mary and Zachariah

In a carefully crafted theological move, Luke contrasts this little story, sandwiched between the larger story of John the Baptist's conception and birth, with Zachariah the priest from the hill country and Mary the maiden from obscure Nazareth. In setting up this antithesis, Luke

---

17. Gula, *Call to Holiness*, 135.

perhaps intends to show that God upsets human understanding of importance of place and person.

In early verses of the chapter, Zachariah had encountered the angel Gabriel, one of two angels mentioned by name in the Bible. Michael (Dan 10:13; 12:1) is the other. Gabriel's name means God is my hero/warrior. This most important personage in the chapter, last appeared to Daniel in the Old Testament to give him "understanding" (Dan 9:21). Like unto Mary, the angel spoke also to Zachariah. Luke contrasts Mary's response with that of Zachariah. Where Zachariah responds "How shall I know . . . "? Mary asks "How can this be . . . ?" The fundamental difference in the two responses: "know" and "be" reveals a deeper reality regarding disposition.

Suffice it to say that perhaps the real difference between the two is that Zachariah wanted a sign. On the other hand, by wanting to know how it can be, Mary has already disposed herself to participate. She wanted to know the extent to which she can engage and be present. While Zachariah had the paraphernalia of Jewish patriarchal culture, Mary represents the biblical *anawim*, the poor, seeking God's deliverance. Yet, the former received divine reprisal for his doubt, and the latter divine approval for her active engagement. Mary celebrates her approval in prophesy in the home of the mute-stricken priest, Zachariah, his wife Elizabeth, and their unborn child. Ironically, in this Lukan narrative, Zachariah, the priest, remained silent while the two women, Elizabeth and Mary, spoke, even the infant in the womb, leapt. Elizabeth cries out, Mary proclaims (Luke 1: 42ff). They both cried and proclaimed the newness, the possibilities of God. Annunciation of abundant life and denunciation of injustice converge in this liberative song, the *Magnificat*. One can discern from the *Magnificat* the theme of alternative community that both critiques and energizes the dominant community. This song represents the new beginnings. The impossible became possible for the young woman from anonymity. A female prophetic voice was also an impossibility in the climate of that day.

Reversals represent the impossibility of God, "For nothing is impossible with God." The miracle of Elizabeth's pregnancy demonstrates the power of God. Even in the Hebrew Scriptures, God's power of reversal is manifest in the cases of Sarah the mother of Isaac, the unnamed mother of Samson (Judg 13: 2–25), and Hannah the mother of Samuel. Of much interest represents the fact that Mary's *Magnificat* in Luke is based on the biblical tradition of the song of Hannah in I Samuel. In these cases, the

American theologian, Thomas C. Oden explained that God made the impossible birth possible, by elevating the lowly to put down the rich and the mighty.[18] Moreover, Joel Rosenberg's claim, that the many turns of personal and familial fortune in the ensuing chapters of the books of Samuel are an elaboration of the compressed strophes of Hannah's song,[19] can also be said of the rest of the Gospel of Luke. Luke's Gospel is consistent with lifting up and bringing to the fore those on the margins.

The seeming impossibility became ever more possible at the second instance of voice. In verse 38, Mary took the center stage. A hitherto invisible frightened young woman self-proclaims: *idou h doulē kyriou· genoito moi kata to rhma sou*, (Here your servant LORD, or "At Your Service, My LORD," my translation.) By designating and claiming servant-hood, Mary expresses her lowly condition before Israel's Adonai, who is her *kyriou*.[20] Her notion of *being* the LORD's servant and *belonging* to that same LORD, grounds her self-understanding.

This conscious and intimate sense of God derived from the assurance of Divine assistance. By her *fiat*, Mary casts her lot with Israel's matriarchs, *doulas*, women who enabled God's salvation plan to happen in Israel's history. Verse 38, the pivotal point in the narrative represents the essence of the Good News: that the disenfranchised can partake of the very nature of God. A paradigm shift occurs. By this shift, something totally new occurs, a new maiden has been born, a Handmaid not of men, but of the LORD—*doulē kyriou*.

Mary's total commitment to servant-hood reveals her as responsible and responsive to the divine presence in her life. Her responsiveness expressed in self-gift represents an ascending response to God's descending gift. The act of self-gift or self-sacrifice expresses the deepest possession of dignity, for only one with dignity can give of one's self. Mary's ability to say "yes" demonstrates a faith grounded in the tradition of her people. She was acutely aware of her bond to the people of Israel in her own generation, a bond which extends back to Abraham and Sara.[21] In rights idiom, therefore, Mary's self-designated role, slave of the LORD, validates the testimony in verse 34. Such testimony comes

---

18. Oden, *Word of Life*, 137. See also, Fitzmyer, G*ospel According to Luke*, 337–334; Johnson, *Truly Our Sister*, 249.

19. Rosenberg, "1 and 2 Samuel," 124.

20. Fitzmyer, *Gospel According to Luke*, 350.

21. Frizzell, "Mary and the Biblical Heritage," 30.

The Handmaid: Mary of Nazareth 53

as a truth "from below" in the face of stronger truth that is from the position of social power. This self-proclamation of slavehood of the LORD in effect transfers Mary's allegiance from Joseph, a representative of patriarchy, on the one hand, to the LORD, on the other hand. Mary's freedom in professing servanthood secures her a place in God's household. In antiquity, the status of a slave was determined by the status of the householder, so "in characterizing Mary of Nazareth as 'slave of the LORD,' Luke has begun to undercut the competitive maneuvering for positions of status prevalent in the first-century Mediterranean world."[22] Such maneuvering of position is prevalent even in contemporary Church life and society. In announcing the Good News to Mary, therefore, the angel Gabriel simultaneously denounces injustice that sustains the maneuvering for positions.

Mary gains full liberty through the very act of expressing her *fiat*. The extraordinary act enables Mary to make her "cross-over," the self-gift, "Here I am," with no intermediaries!

That Mary makes her crossing without an intermediary suggests that she acts as responsible moral agent. At the moment of encounter, there was neither Joseph nor any of the patriarchal structures which marked the beginning of her journey to carry her past the threshold. Mary of Nazareth accomplished the act on her own. Like her foremother, Israel's *doulas*, she takes responsibility and personally makes this self-offering to God. Thus in Mary's *fiat*, Luke makes an alternative statement about gender and its institutions. The alternative represents a reimagined way of relationship, a relationship based on service as the overriding experience of living in the family of God. Service sets aside all manners of domination based on patriarchal and on special knowledge or gift.[23]

By her self-gift, Mary enters into a bilateral covenantal relationship with God. She matches God's descending gift with her ascending response. She places herself at God's command. Mary not only submits; she expresses her agreement with the divine gift. "Her human response appertains to history (*idou*, "here") and not to an abstract ontology (*eimi*, "I am"). Like Jesus before his passion (22:14) or Paul in view of his fate (Acts 21:14), Mary awaits the fulfillment of God's will, a divine history written not in the letters of the Scriptures but in the life of the

---

22. Green, *Gospel of Luke*, 92.
23. Uzukwu, *Listening Church*, 136.

people."²⁴Evidently, this second instance of voicing is self-defining, liberative, and cathartic. Voice proclaims a person as a conscious being capable of independent thought and action in ongoing history.

In the next several centuries that follow the birth of Christianity, the act of self-offering would become one of the most liberative tools for Christian women of the era. Women in early Christianity, particularly in North Africa, Syria, and Persia obtained freedom from patriarchal control by their self-gift to God. By declaring themselves virgins for life, they give themselves over to service in the community an action consistent with that of the *doulas kyriou*. Their self-offer freed them from the obligation of marriage and family to devote themselves to service in the churches.²⁵ It may sound ironic given that Mary starts a family at the instigation of her vocation, but the case in point is self-gift. Mary gave herself for service, and that service was to be the mother of the Redeemer. A sense of devotion allowed Mary to embrace the purpose of God unreservedly. She attempts to match God's generosity by giving without counting the cost to her personally. When one considers the social impact of an unwed pregnant Jewish teenager in first century Palestine, one begins to realize that Mary's acceptance to serve was unto death. She was risking her life, possibly getting stoned or banished for her pregnancy, or potentially dying in childbirth. Like the prophet Isaiah who responds to the question "who will go for us," with the words: "Here I am . . . Send me" in Isaiah 6:8, Mary, sucked into the realm of God, lets out the prophetic response, "*idou h doulē kyriou· genoito moi kata to rhma sou idou doulē kyriou*. Mary emerges as a prophet. Luke puts in Mary's mouth a prophetic utterance, words of discipleship, servant words, "Here I am send me", "I come to do your will," "Behold, I am the handmaid of the Lord" (v. 38; cf. Isa 6:8; cf. Heb. 10:7, Luke 1:38). Mary understood herself as chosen to be a disciple of God, and as a disciple, a servant and a leader, in the sense that the Master is a leader and a disciple can be as good as the master. This female servant meets Isaiah's characterization of the "Servant of the Lord," one chosen, endowed with the spirit, humble, and compassionate.

New Testament exegetes are ever slow to apply the term "servant of the LORD" to Mary of Nazareth although that was how she understood herself, *doulē kyriou*. These scholars fail to recognize fully that

---

24. Bovon, *Luke 1*, 53.
25. Irvin and Sunquist, *History of the World Christian Movement*, 150.

for thirty years, Jesus, *doulos kyriou*, the Servant of the LORD, lived in obedience to his mother, *doulē kyriou*, in Nazareth. In Mary's hearth, Jesus advanced in wisdom and age within a nurturing community. Put differently, the son's servant-hood emerged from lessons from his mother's hearth. Mary's relationship with Jesus reminds me of the role of the mother of the seven young men in the Fourth Book of Maccabees. In this story, the unnamed mother encouraged each of her seven children in the "language of their ancestors," that metaphoric mother tongue, to fidelity to the Law, to sacrifice for the common good. The self-gift of Jesus unto death influences the Christian notion of *diakonia*. Christians individually and collectively bear united witness to the service unto death of Mary of Nazareth and her Son, Jesus. Invariably, self-gift remains the central message of the passage, "Be it done unto me according to your Word;" self-gift is possible only for one who possesses dignity.

Having accomplished the liberation of the maiden from Nazareth, the angel departs, leaving Mary on her own. But she was not without the most powerful advocate, the Holy Spirit. The Spirit continues the transformation. Moved by the Holy Spirit, Mary proceeds from the scene of encounter to the hill country of Judea. Like the prophet, she had the Word "burning like a fire in" her heart "imprisoned in her bones" and she could not hold it in (Jer 20:9). Off she went to the hill country to proclaim the greatness of the Lord who lifts up the lowly from the dust (Luke 1:39ff). In proclaiming, she redefines the dominant version of social reality, announcing God's alternative community as the *Magnificat* portends. The *Magnificat* (Luke 1:46–55) tradition can be understood as a poetic, imaginative practice of the textual tradition of the song of Hannah (1 Sam 2:1–10). God's alternative community confronts the dominant culture, particularly the culture that proclaims might as ethically just. God's greatness is manifest in the divine capability to bring about justice to the world. Evidently, no one touched by God's Spirit remains the same. Transformed, Mary grounds her experience in active ministry, she went with haste to serve and proclaim God's word. That is the character of the transformed Nazareth maiden, the Handmaid of the LORD. The glorification of Mary, therefore, as the ultimate model of women's submission flies in the face of her self-understanding as an active participant in her contemporary history.

Ideology: Discipleship

Whose handmaid is Mary of Nazareth? A response to this inquiry directs critical attention to the narrative. It asks whose story is being told in Luke 1:26–38. The inquiry allows one to seek out who has the dominant role in the episode. William C. Spohn points out that tensions and reversals of plot gradually define the central characters over the course of the story.[26] In this case, Mary represents the unquestionable central character of the Annunciation episode. In African cultural idiom, the dominant voice in a story represents the voice of the ancestor. Evidence in the passage suggests that Mary remains the unquestionably dominant voice, and therefore, the ancestor in the narrative. For some, the idea of placing a female's experience and subjectivity at the center of the Annunciation episode may appear unorthodox. Perhaps placing a female at the heart of the story of the Incarnation represents an attempt at presenting the feminine face of God. Or else, the female presence challenges readers to note the deeper meaning of the Incarnation. If that was not the case, why in the world would a female character dominate the story? Again the story demonstrates that the female is unquestionably the first human person, in the new dispensation, to handle holy things on behalf of God.

The Annunciation narrative in its foundation represents the story of women. Claiming this story as women's tale is secured in its being a birth narrative. Normally, birth stories are told either by or of women. Since the incarnation is about God becoming one with us, it follows that God chose our mode of communication to communicate the God-self.

Still at this level, the narrative can function as a paradigm for evangelization. It is significant that the Greek word for Annunciation translates *euangelismos*, evangelization, indicating that this Lukan passage functions as a prime example of evangelization. Here, Luke tells anew God's liberating power from *the below* in Mary's *Magnificat*. Told from the point of view of the disenfranchised, the one *below* makes the Lukan narrative a testimony.

The testimony lays bare, as well as breaks, conventional assumptions and gives a new perspective of the Word. Because of the testimony, women can redream and reimagine the world. Such witness invites readers and hearers to another imagination of the world, a world under God.

---

26. Spohn, *Go and Do Likewise*, 29.

Only under God's rule, can an unmarried young village maiden undergo a radical transformation in a society that is strongly patriarchal. Mary's active involvement is consistent with the freedom of participation that characterizes Israel's *doulas*. For this *doulē kyriou*, the relevant question was not *who* am I? But *Whose* am I? A response shows that she has been claimed by God so that her destiny is bound up with others.[27] The theology here is that of engagement and not of individual salvation. Since relationality favors African women's way of engagement, they can identify with Mary's sense of relationality and solidarity that her question, *how can this be...* suggests and which her visit to Elizabeth and Zachariah confirms. Sharing, engendered and rooted in solidarity, becomes even more intense for one so highly favored. Such favors evoke greater commitment, a commitment to engage the world and explore new horizons with and for others.

Engaging the world as *doulē* challenges women to reread Scripture contextually. Active engagement with the sacred text challenges African women to work for a more integral participation of women in society and church life. Such exercise allows women to challenge interpretations that tend to marginalize and subjugate. Critical engagement with Scripture enables women to enter into texts finding meaning that unburdens and uplifts their humanity. Such reading facilitates transformation, and brings positive changes into the individual and to the community. Like the *doulas* of old, African women's quest for healing and community and the strength to carry on through wars, deprivation and famine, is profoundly other-worldly but profoundly this-worldly too. African Christian women's religiosity has deep roots. Their religiosity emerges from traditional religiosity. These, combined with a sharper sense of female dignity, social purpose and personal piety culled from Bible and ecclesiastical practice, enable them move forward.[28] These positive values demand recognition and reinforcement. But some African women scholars rather than supporting these positive values continue to sustain the idea of women's subordination through a poor interpretation of the Handmaid.

Regardless of Luke's characterization of Mary as *doulē kyriou*, some women scholars continue to buttress the idea of the Handmaid as *paidiskē*. These scholars interpret Mary's *fiat* as passivity and unques-

27. Spohn, *Go and Do Likewise*, 163.
28. Hastings, *Church in Africa*, 51.

tioning submission. A synchronic reading of the text reveals Mary's act of obedience as listening obedience, and her openness towards future explanation and fulfillment. For Mary's obedience is not portrayed merely in passive terms. This Nazareth woman expresses active acceptance and positive response. By her self-description as *doulē kyriou*, Mary acknowledges her submission to God's purpose, and her role in assisting that purpose. In this episode, Luke paints a scene of a community of love and yields to submission. The divine messenger, Gabriel, did not force God's will on Mary. Love does not do that. Genuine relationship is marked by submission as the suggestion of the Trinitarian presence in verse 35 implies. Indeed, submission is all about relationship of love and respect. It is not about authority or obedience. Mary's submission to the divine will has been problematic for some.

Men are not the only ones who employ Mary's act of submission as an instrument of oppression against women. Women, particularly representatives of patriarchy who may be leaders of women's communities are not different from the men. Inherent in the patriarchal notion of obedience is the servant-slave model. This servant-slave representation reinforces the colonial mentality and stifles initiative for the mission. Under such regulation, a religious woman never questions. She must obey promptly, she is told, "like Mary!" This practice grossly undermines the dialogical relationship found in the annunciation passage. Nothing in the passage suggests that Mary obeyed promptly. How can anyone overlook the fact that it is in dialogue the Word became Flesh? "God's reign breaks into the world through specific conversations, confrontations, and decisions of actual people."[29] Undoubtedly, the servant-slave mode in which Mary is placed paves the way for fideism. In other words, the attitude becomes "whatever they say, or decide that I will do, God will take care"; "they," meaning the community leaders. Unfortunately, when Sisters or any group of women, can no longer make informed decision about their lives, the community itself ceases to exist in the proper sense of the word. The stifling of initiatives and barring Sisters from active participation hits at the very foundation of the Incarnation story. In order to recover the proper sense of mission therefore, we as religious must interpret for ourselves our Scripture, and make our own agenda. We must reject the burden of a name that is not truly ours. A continuous acceptance of the Handmaid as a model of submissiveness resonates

---

29. Spohn, *Go and Do Likewise*, 127.

with Iwuchukwu's reading of the Annunciation pericope. She proposes women's dependence on patriarchal authority. Such dependence often leads to distrust of one's own authority and experience, and knowledge.

Iwuchukwu's assertion that African women learn from Mary the act of submission and sacrifice demands analysis. It does appear that Iwuchukwu's understanding of sacrifice is suggestive of self-immolation. The very act of self-immolation represents an act against human dignity. Sacrifice in its foundation is redemptive. Nigerian theologian Teresa Okure lifts the redemptive aspect of sacrifice stating that "through sacrifice, humans seek to encounter the divine, project themselves into the invisible world, penetrate into the divine presence and commune with the deity."[30] This notion of sacrifice creates a bridge between humans and God.

Essentially, sacrifice constitutes a need to cooperate with the divine plan. The *doulē kyriou* cooperate with God's plan in fostering salvation and redemption, communion, and reconciliation. Mary cooperates with God to restore dignity to humankind.

Iwuchukwu encourages Nigerian Christian women's exploitation and non-participation in life's processes. Essentially, she expects women to become mules. The exploitative and oppressive reading of Mary's obedience to the divine command furthers patriarchal hegemony. Mary's *Magnificat* challenges such power. The African woman in Iwuchukwu's perception remains utterly passive, an empty vessel waiting to be filled by her husband or representatives of patriarchy in women's religious communities.

The American exegete Joel Green offers a more positive image of the *doulē* in the household. Green states that Mary's claim to a place in God's household in her socio-historical context, actually placed in jeopardy Mary's status in Joseph's household. In this sense, partnership in the purpose of God transcends the claims of family.[31] This interpretation uncovers the employment of gender and divine representation. Creating a positive image of women in God's household requires an employment of the imagination. Only at the level of the imagination, Amos wilder states, can any full engagement with life take place. The kind of imagination that facilitates positive change represents that which Wilder described as a necessary component of all profound knowing

30. Okure, 'Hebrews: Sacrifice in an African Perspective," 535.
31. Green, *Gospel of Luke*, 92.

and celebration; all remembering, realizing, and anticipating; all faith, hope, and love.[32] This kind of imagination sustains doctrine. Wilder insists that when imagination fails, doctrine becomes ossified, witness and proclamation wooden, doxologies and litanies empty, consolations hollow, and ethics legalistic.[33] Could this be what is happening to women in African society and church life? Without doubt, positive imagination provides the tools to dream dreams and produce language that will facilitate liberative processes, as well as the growth of the humanity of both men and women.

The liberative process is connected fundamentally with voice. Twice in the Annunciation narrative, the voice of Mary comes to life. In the first instance, she reacts or rather questions, the angel's life-altering message *"pws estai tou to, epei andra ou ginwskw;* (Luke 1:34). Second, she articulates her self-understanding, embodied in her *fiat—Idou h doulē kyriou· genoito moi kata to rhma sou* (Luke 1:38). Mary's voice in the text denies the muteness associated with submissiveness often ascribed to the handmaid of the Annunciation. Her voice in the passage supports and corroborates characteristics of the *doulas* in the Septuagint. Like her maternal ancestors, by speaking Mary demonstrates that women did have space, freedom of action, and self-determination as well as possessing, within a context undeniably patriarchal, status and dignity.

Mary responds and acts on God's word like a disciple who hears the master's voice. To hear the word of God and act on it represents the foundational mode of Israel's religion embodied in the Shema: "Hear, O Israel! The LORD is our God, the LORD alone! . . . " (Deut 6:4–9; 11:13–21; Num 15:37–41). The Shema is also very resonant with the Israelite struggle for autonomy in the face of external forces, particularly against a threat to monotheism.

Scholars identify hearing and acting upon God's word as that which marks a genuine disciple in Luke's theology. Hearing the Word and acting on it reveals the eschatological vocation of discipleship, which the *doulē kyriou* signifies.[34] Thus, hearing the word and keeping it draws one into a covenantal relationship that Jesus' community represents (Luke 11:28). Mary, a member of this new covenant community, broke a cultural taboo to become a progenitor of the new people of God born of

32. Wilder, *Theopoetic Theology*, 2.
33. Wilder, *Theopoetic Theology*.
34. Fitzmyer, *Anchor Bible*, 341.

the Spirit. The Pentecost event actualized the new People of God (Acts 2). Pentecost symbolizes a liberative event for the individual Christian and the community of believers. Luke presents women and men in the Pentecost event as God's faithful partners in new community (Acts 2:14–21 citing Joel 2:28–32).

> *kai ge epi tous doulous mou kai epi tas doulas mou en tais hmerais ekeinais ekcew apo tou pneumatos mou, kai profhteusousin* (Acts 2:18).
>
> Indeed, upon my servants and my handmaids I will pour out a portion of my spirit in those days, and they shall prophesy (Translation, *The Catholic Study Bible*, Second Edition).

Interestingly, the *doulas* in this Pentecost passage emerge on equal footing with the *doulos*. In placing the male servants and female servants alongside each other, the author establishes the model for living in the age of the Spirit.

In similar vein, the apostle Peter emphasizes that the reestablished people of God include women and men. Peter's utterance strongly affirms the equal value of persons in the new dispensation. Through a repeated gender differentiation, the quotation from Joel is evidence that when God pours out his Spirit in the last days, it will be without respect to gender.[35] Only this common share in the Spirit renders eschatological legitimation. Hence, Luke insists on the *doulē* expressiveness in the epoch of life in the Spirit (cf. Acts 2:18).

The voice of the *doulas* in the new dispensation challenges a popular Nigerian saying "if you want something said, tell a man. If you want something done, tell a woman." Without doubt, in this era, a woman can speak on behalf of herself and on behalf of others. Speaking has never been the preserve of men, just as doing is not just the prerogative of women. Luke's women continue to speak even at the end of his Gospel narrative: "Then the [women] returned from the tomb and announced all these things to the eleven and to all the other" (Luke 24:9).

The prophetic role of Luke's *doulas* call up images of prophets in the Hebrew Scriptures: Servant of God, leader, bridge-builder, advocate, and most significantly, a voice for the people. By dressing the *doulē* in a prophet's robe, and placing her at the beginning of Luke's Gospel and at the beginning of the Church (Acts 2), the author points to the liberative

---

35. Seim, *Double Message*, 51.

potential the Good News heralds. Indeed, exploring pneumatic resources in the Bible will facilitate women's discovering that the "Pentecost story contains the story of the conscientization of women" and that the mission of Pentecost involves both men and women as co-laborers and joint heirs as members of God's new *ekklesia*.[36] To engage the world as *doulē* offers transformation that makes possible living fully in the Spirit (Acts 2:18).

To live fully in the Spirit implies a prophetic existence. Women's prophetic voices in the world must be heard in the context of disenabling oppressive religious and cultural structures. In living the life of the Spirit, which the *doulos* and *doulas* suggest, women in Africa, indeed, every woman can claim a prophetic role. This claim also can provide the key that unlocks the female's muteness, drawing her out from the shadows into visibility and active participation.

Conclusion

The concept of the *doulē* in the biblical tradition offers liberative elements. Through the agency of transformation, liberative potential in the metaphor of the *doulē* moves and frees persons from situations of powerlessness. Such energy places a person in a redeemed situation of empowerment that secures dignity and makes self-gift possible. The liberating power of the Spirit, manifested in the Pentecost event, transforms God's *doulous* and *doulas* from servitude for service, service for the revitalization of the community. But such transformation is ineffectual with inattentiveness to the Holy Spirit. It is the presence of the Holy Spirit that authenticates the community of believers. To attain freedom, women like Mary of Nazareth must embrace unconditionally the transforming power of the Spirit. Women must free themselves of and from the concept of handmaid as *paidiskē*. In this respect, a radical reappropriation of the Annunciation passage offers the key that allows women to engage the world as servant-leaders. Understanding oneself, as servant-leader, therefore, remains essentially liberative. Thus, the *doulē* metaphor becomes inspirational for women's struggle in male-dominated contemporary many African societies.

Roman Catholic tradition's appropriation of certain *doulē* characteristics for the Cult of the Virgin Mary, underscores the essential

---

36. Kalu, "Daughters of Ethiopia," 275.

qualities of the *doulē*, service in leadership. Service in leadership embraces the context in which African women theologize. With such overwhelming evidence, it behooves African women to disallow depiction of themselves as naturally inferior, subordinate, and eternal victims of male oppression. In so doing, they can engage the world as *doulē*, visible and active participants in ongoing history. In the Gospel, Jesus institutes the memorial of his presence among believers in the context of service, "For who is greater: the one seated at table or the one who serves? Is it not the one seated at table? I am among you as the one who serves" (Luke 22:27; John 13:4–16). Thus the Good news is that greatness resides in the willingness to be servants and not to be served (Matt 20:20–28). This fundamental understanding of Christianity universalizes the *doulē* metaphor.

The call to service and faithful discipleship extends to women and men alike. Those who become servants or slaves, *doulas, douloi* represent the truly great. The *doulas* service function renews and revitalizes the society, providing an exemplary significance for the whole community and for its leadership. The newness the Spirit brings into the lives of people confirms the transformative message of this Lukan passage.[37] In this regard, appropriating the notion of *doulē* allows women to break away from the tutelage the functional interpretation of the "handmaid" imposes. The creative power of the Holy Spirit liberates. The newness the Spirit brings into the lives of people confirms the transformative message of this Lukan passage. Most especially, the narrative awakens new hope, a hope that another world is possible for the disenfranchised. Other norms besides Scripture can be liberative. Tradition, common human moral standards, and prophetic voices in community represent sources where a people can find meaning that unburdens and uplifts their humanity. We look to the next chapter for these other sources.

---

37. Seim, *Double Message*, 96, 97.

4

The Power of Naming in African-Igbo Culture

Nkolika: Recalling-Is-Greatest.[1]
—CHINUA ACHEBE

Introduction

There was an Old Testament prophet who named his son The remnant-shall-return. They must have lived in times like this. We have a different metaphor, though; we have our own version of hope that springs eternal. We shall call this child AMAECHINA: May-the-path-never-close.[2]

IN IGBO SOCIETY, STORIES take different forms. Personal names represent one such form. In this society, names are powerful symbols, words that act as markers. For this same reason, the freight that the name designation Handmaid carries cannot be underestimated. Certain female names, however, remain connected to structures that perpetuate women's subordination in Igbo society. This way of naming resonates with the designation "Handmaid," which I covered in Chapter two.

Drawing on the biblical tradition of the *doulē*, my story shows that certain female names employed to construct and silence women can be redemptive. Moreover, the claim of cultural affinity between the Igbo and the land of the Bible suggests that the idea of the biblical *doulē* has currency for the Igbo. This claim raises legitimate questions concerning women in Igbo society. Does the similarity between both cultures relate only to patriarchal mores? Or does it also suggest that *doulas* figures

1. Achebe, *Anthills* 124.
2. Achebe, *Anthills*, 222.

inhabit Igbo Society? A close reading of the biblical text suggests that the context of the biblical *doulas* depicts a similar circumstance of women in Igbo society: family, community, hope, mutuality, reciprocity, justice, oppression, peace, war, and patriarchal structure. Evidently, in the end, Igbo-Hebrew cultural affiliation may indeed provide the key to reading women's role in Igbo society, a role which pejorative or inane names tend to obscure. In this way, the name as a story becomes critical to the gender discourse.

The present narrative engages the textual tradition and the living tradition of female names. Examining the tradition and some contemporary women's names reveals the implication of name and naming. Interviewing women about female names has revealed that some women believe that debasing female names belong to the past. Women who think that debasing names are things of the past remain truly unaware of how much that past influences contemporary relations. But unbecoming names are not totally of the past, because what is rent asunder does not have the integrity to provide a complete vessel for its history. Inappropriate names, past or contemporary, continue to support the ideology that foster women's subjugation in cultures that place significance on name designation. When someone has a name where integrity leaks every time they are called to identity awareness, how much agency can be expected?

While interrogating cultural name texts that shrink women's horizons and hinder them from recognizing their full potential, the story I tell in this chapter seeks liberative insights from Igbo historical past, symbols that always have been vehicles for redemptive honesty. The retrieval processes brings to the fore the fear and pain that individuals want so desperately to share, to own, but have lacked the means, or rather have not been permitted, to do. In this way, this project becomes a prophetic undertaking.

This narrative unfolds in two stages. First it uncovers and recovers structures that enervate women's participation in life's processes. The second stage reconstructs, reweaves those structures or strands in such a way that they can become liberative. Retrieval of positive elements obfuscated by patriarchy, colonialism, sexism, androcentrism, and missionary proselytism constitutes an integral part of the present undertaking.[3] I employ the term sexism to represent that which obscures the analysis

3. Bujo, *African Theology*, 130.

of historical reality. The study of sexism in the historical discourse reveals the biases of patriarchal history. The use of the term androcentrism represents a world construction in language that legitimates patriarchy.[4] And patriarchy represents the rule of the fathers. The rule entails the systematic exclusion of women from the public sphere by legal, political and economic arrangements which operate to favor men.[5]

Having introduced the discussion, the rest of the chapter divides into two major sections. Section one provides the ground for the significance of naming in an African-Igbo milieu by focusing on three subsections, storytelling, metaphor, and the significance of name and naming in sub-Sahara Africa. Section two concentrates on the subject of deconstruction and reconstruction of female names. It employs the novels *Anthills of the Savannah* and *Bread Givers* as well as reflections from interview subjects.[6] The prophetic stance I take in this narrative is from the prophecy of Jeremiah 1:10. The prophetic tearing down and rebuilding describes the deconstruction and reconstruction used in this narrative to facilitate the reimaging of women in contemporary Igbo society. The process of deconstructing and constructing draws on storytelling, stories that reveal the sacredness of life, stories that point to events that have hurt and healed, events that have given life and death.

Retelling: The Significance of Story

African religious anthropology provides the tools for reconstructing women's role. Scholarly inquiry into African religious anthropology continues to occupy the interest of contemporary African women theologians. African women theologians, led by Ghanaian theologian Mercy Amba Oduyoye, are undertaking the task of retelling women's stories.[7] Oduyoye, whose anthropologic-theological vision attempts to retell women's stories in her writings does so "not only to undermine the androcentric and patriarchal [mis]interpretation of the feminine modality of humanity, but also to retrieve in theological terms what it means to be truly human."[8] The retelling of women's stories aim at making sense out

---

4. Schüsler Fiorenza, "Breaking the Silence," 162.
5. Avis, *Eros and the Sacred*, 10.
6. Achebe, *Anthills* and Yezierska, *Bread Givers*.
7. Oduyoye, *Daughters of Anowa*, 16.
8. Dedji, *Reconstruction & Renewal*, 29.

of their experience of chaos, institutionalized by centuries of domestication. Retelling women's stories attempts to call society back to its divine origins by fostering human dignity. Chinua Achebe insightfully captures the essence of storytelling in the term: *nkolika,* recalling-is-greatest,

> It is the story . . . that saves our progeny from blundering like blind beggars into the spikes of the cactus fence. The story is our escort; without it, we are blind. Does the blind man own his escort? No, neither do we the story; rather it is the story that owns us and directs us. It is the thing that makes us different from cattle; it is the mark on the face that sets one people apart from their neighbors.[9]

The normative role of stories in the African oral corpus can be cathartic and therapeutic. The form of storytelling provides constructive tools for the future. For the retrieval and celebration of women's positive image to have meaning, there must be a remembrance, a memory, continuity, and a story.

Story-telling as a form of remembrance unmasks critically and it creatively opens people's eyes so that by remembering, they can see, understand and believe (cf. Luke 1:4). Besides, remembrance, stories represent the anamnestic role of the community in which the memory of the people resides. Thus, the exemplary values of narratives retain their power for the present. African stories, not unlike biblical stories, represent both responsive and assertive means that make them remain deeply imaginative. The validity of story lies in its power to proclaim a social reality.[10] That is to say, stories announce a particular way of life, which raw facts thickly or thinly veil. In this sense, stories give women as well as men the paradigm for theological reflection.

African women theologians attempt to redeem non-liberative stories of women. Their sensitivity to theological issues emerges from lived experience in ongoing history, and their critique of oppression focuses on intuitional structures such as marriage, kinships, and other forms of gender relations.[11] Engaging these macro-issues has inspired other theological enterprises. This narrative, however, continues the women's story from a micro-perspective. It engages those innocuous social issues that

---

9. Achebe, *Anthills*, 124.

10. Brueggemann, *Word Militant*, 91.

11. Njoroge, "A New Way of Facilitating Leadership: Lessons from African Women Theologians," 395.

escape critical scrutiny, yet remain indispensable in social construction. These matters represent the building blocks or root metaphors utilized in the gender construction. Constructions of certain female names practically objectifies or essentialize the female. American biblical scholar Judy Siker highlights the tension between essentialism and non-essentialism inherent in gender construction. "Essentialism suggests that there is one clear set of characteristics that all members of the group share across time. Non-essentialism, on the other hand, suggests that in addition to common characteristics, there are characteristics that not only differ but also change and change radically according to time and situation."[12] Siker further states that this "tension can be seen in theories contrasting biological and social constructionist approaches or contrasting the idea of identity as a fixed, trans-historical concept versus a fluid, contingent construct."[13] In Siker's view, and as I show, identity is not something uncovered so much as constructed. Certain names given to a female child in Igbo society constitute one such root metaphor employed in identity construction.

As root metaphors, names represent more than a convenient collocation of sounds by which a person could be identified. Rather a name expresses something of the essence of that which was being named, an understanding, which derives from the Igbo "world-sense."[14] The term "world-sense" is a creation of African feminist scholars.[15] These scholars coin the term to replace the term "worldview." They interpret worldview as a Western concept that tends to privilege the visual. The reason the body has so much presence in the West, according to this notion, is the fact that the world primarily is perceived by sight, hence, the nomenclature, worldview. World-sense, on the other hand, represents an attempt to capture the manner in which Africans engage the world. Theologically expressed, I believe this to be the intersection of cosmology and anthropology. Africa's foremost scholar of religion, John Mbiti, affirms that Africans engage all five major senses to make sense of their experiences. "All their five major senses were open gates through which all kinds of experiences [came] upon them. These experiences stimulated them to

---

12. Siker, "Unmasking the Enemy: Deconstructing the "Other" in the Gospel of Matthew," 111.

13. Siker, "Unmasking the Enemy."

14. Oyewumi, "Visualizing the Body: Western Theories and African Subjects," 4–5.

15. Oyewumi, "Visualizing the Body."

reflect upon their life and the universe in which they lived. The result was a gradual building up of African views of ideas about the world and the universe at large.[16] This sense perception, intertwined with the fundamental understanding of divine reality, stimulated Africans to reflect upon their life and the universe in which they live. Stories represent a basic form of communicating such life experiences.

Stories encapsulated in personal names represent cultural texts, whose textual qualities blend with other strands, to produce certain images of women that continue to prove non-liberative. I use text to include not only the traditional written word which affects humans and culture, but in addition documents, symbols, visual arts, social systems, and the myths which maintain them.

The evocation of names as metaphors draws on imaginative reading of this cultural text. Because the freight a name text carries include a wide semantic range, the language of metaphor becomes a vehicle by which to access its approximate meaning. Thus, neither analytic speech nor the language of coercion can elicit effectively the deepest embodiment of a name. Paul Ricoeur's understanding of metaphor furnishes the critical tool as well as the lens with which to engage name texts.

Metaphor and Cultural Idioms

Ricoeur defines metaphor as symbolic language.[17] This language bears the characteristics of a poem in miniature form, whose uniqueness resides in its figurative meaning. Symbol represents a semantic structure that can have a double-meaning. He further states that the figurative language of metaphor renders it unlike scientific works, whose significance is to be taken literally. Ricoeur posits that the relationship between the literal meaning and the figurative meaning of a metaphor resembles an abridged version with a single sentence of the complex interplay of significations that characterizes the literary work as a whole. A metaphor results from the tension between two terms in a metaphorical utterance. Typically, the tension between the two interpretations sustains a metaphor in existence. Thus a metaphor exists only through an interpretation. "Metaphorical interpretation presupposes a literal interpretation which self-destructs in a significant contradiction. It is this process of

---

16. Mbiti, *An Introduction to African Religion*, 31.
17. Ricoeur, *Interpretation Theory*, 45.

self-destruction or transformation which imposes a sort of twist on the words, an extension of meaning thanks to which we can make sense where a literal interpretation would be literally nonsensical. Hence a metaphor appears as a kind of riposte to a certain inconsistency in the metaphorical utterance literally interpreted."[18] The process of eliciting meaning makes obvious the sense of metaphor. In such usage, metaphor supplements inadequate human language. Because humans possess more ideas than they have words to express, they tend to stretch the signification of those words beyond their ordinary use.

As a rhetorical figure of speech, metaphors aim at making the probable more attractive. As work of discourse, a metaphor brings explicit and implicit meaning to light. Most especially, a metaphor represents the extension of the meaning of a name through deviation from the literal meaning of words.[19] This claim of Igbo names as metaphor derives from the Igbo imagination of the universe. The Igbo live in a symbolic universe and tend to express their experience symbolically. Achebe puts it thus, "Since Igbo people did not construct a rigid and closely argued system of thought to explain the universe and the place of man in it, preferring the metaphor of myth and poetry, anyone seeking an insight into their world must seek it along their own way. Some of these ways are folk tales, proverbs, proper names, rituals, and festivals."[20] The symbolic understanding of name not only permits access into Igbo world and life, it also illumines the role names play in social and identity construction. As a people of oral culture, myths form a greater part of the Igbo self-understanding and their perception of the world.

Myths represent a form of symbolic language that expresses the truths of human existence in a way that rational language cannot. By so doing, the language of myths obliterates any gap in a people's experience of the cosmos. Myth, together with ritual, constitutes what students of language, such as Ricoeur, have called "primary language." As primary language, myths provide the archetype for the construction of identity explicitly or in a subtle manner, especially in societies where religion constitutes a significant and dominant feature in peoples' lives. Creation myths play significant roles in a people's self-understanding of themselves and their universe. The Tanzanian theologian Laurenti Magesa

18. Ricoeur, *Interpretation Theory*, 50.
19. Ricoeur, *Interpretation Theory*, 49.
20. Achebe, "'Chi' in Igbo Cosmology," 67–68.

contends that more than all other myths, cosmogonic myths contain the primordial and pristine moral tradition of any given people.[21] Myths provide a model of the relationship between the sexes and legitimize social institutions and practice in many African societies.

Names that signify ideological constructs share a family resemblance with myths, maxims, idioms, and proverbs on which the community hangs its mores. Myths serve to regulate the community consciousness. Some myths, though, represent structures that hinder women's full participation in life's processes. The task to uncover, recover and reconstruct these structures becomes evident in the community's quest for fullness of life, the flourishing of its members. Such activity involves a prophetic stance that can end the denial and the containment by the dominant culture, a denial that deprives society of the synergy of human potentials. Thus, the prophet must at once evocatively confront enervating structures that weaken the community and establish invigorating and honest configurations that proclaim life. Retelling women's stories provides the foundation for honest assessment and evaluation of women's role in contemporary African and Igboland in particular.

For the Igbo, stories about life provide the framework for interpreting the world. From stories the people can determine factors that impinge on life and how they maintain or disrupt the universal harmony. Women's advancement falls within this range of concern. A cursory review of name and naming in sub-Sahara African and the Igbo in the context highlights the import of a name.

SIGNIFICANCE OF NAME

The African American scholar Alice Walker once wrote, "How simple a thing it seems to me that to know ourselves as we are, we must know our mother's name."[22] Walker's assertion is pertinent to a person's self-understanding. It is this quest for self-understanding that makes imperative a rereading of the Handmaids in the sense of *doulē kyriou*, a self-designate name of Mary of Nazareth.

Walker's forceful claim subtly directs attention to the influence of name on character, and by extension, charism. In this regard, names of religious organizations, family names, as well as given and taken names

21. Magesa, *African Religion*, 36, 43.
22. Walker, *Mother's Garden*, 276.

provide a window into self-understanding of a subject or an organization. Walker's point unearths and calls for an examination of certain Igbo tradition whereby children were known by their mother's name before the advent of Westernization. To know one's mother's name represents a metaphor of existence, an existence that is secured in a mother-child relationship. This relationship emerges from the *mgbala*, the hearth. Perhaps the nomenclature *Nneka*, mother is supreme, derives from a self-understanding that the knowledge of "mother's name" evokes.[23] Similarly, the designation "mother tongue" reveals much about the web of relationships that exists between the mother-child-culture and society.

Because names bear significance on life, their import cannot be ignored. In the Igbo tradition given names represent a family story and taken names also can represent a person's current history. The names of children in an Igbo family frequently tell of the family's hopes, fears, joys, and sorrows. Babies' given names mark circumstances prevailing at the time of conception or birth, and in this way, names constitute a kind of oral history. Besides, a name becomes so important that it largely corresponds to the particular unique personality. Names are not only symbolic; they link the child to the ancestors and indicate the origin of one's personality.[24] Hence, to know someone's name means knowing something of the fundamental traits, nature, or destiny of the name-bearer.[25] To have knowledge of someone's name may also mean to have some exercise of power of them. In a similar vein, most biblical names have deeper meanings and can function as metaphor. A few examples would suffice.

In Genesis 32:31, the one who struggles with Jacob refuses to reveal his name; perhaps to protect identity. Similarly, the name of the "event" Moses encounters at the scene of the burning bush yields a whole religious and historical phenomenon. "I am who am" (Exod 3:14). The "I am who am" goes further to reveal other details of the self: "The LORD, the God of your fathers, the God of Abraham, the God of Isaac, the God of Jacob . . . This is my name forever; this is my title for all generations" (Exod 3:15). Other biblical names include Moses, "I drew him out

23. Chinweizu, *Anatomy of Female Power*, 114.

24. Nasimiyu-Wasike, "Christianity and the African Rituals of Birth and Naming," 48.

25. Bohmbach, "Name and Naming," 944.

of the water" (Exod 2:10), Samuel, the mother, "had asked the Lord of him" (1 Sam 1:20), Nabal, "fool" (1 Sam 25:25), and most striking are the names of the three children of the prophet Hosea and his wife Gomer: Jezreel, Lo-ruhama, and Lo-ammi (Hos 1: 3–8), symbolic names that foreshadow doom for idolatrous Israel. In the New Testament, the name of Jesus (Luke 1:31–33) tells of a metaphor *par excellence*. The name of Jesus appears to be synonymous with the person of Jesus both in his humanity and divinity.

The New Testament writers generously underscored the unique personality that the name of Jesus conveys. In Luke 10:7, for example, on returning from their first mission, the seventy (two) disciples testify to their master that "even the demons are subject to us because of your name." In the Gospel of Mark, demons try to get a handle on Jesus' power by naming him, but he silenced them (Mark 3:11–12). Acts 3: 6 narrates the story of Peter and John healing the crippled beggar in the name of Jesus. The Apostle Paul insists that "at the name of Jesus every knee should bow" (Phil 2:10). Equating a name with a person is replete in the Hebrew Scriptures, particularly in the Psalms. Evidently, among the Semites as among the Igbo, names represent a metaphor of a person. Consequently, names have a sacred character and must be chosen and given cautiously.

For most Africans, to call a person's name without a good reason dishonors her or him. American longtime missionary in West Africa, Del Tarr observes that "Names of individuals are not used in greetings like: 'Hello, John, how are you today?' Names are simply not used easily, even between friends. A name possesses an aura and an essence of power related to 'life-force.'"[26] Names appear to represent something mysterious, something felt as being the actual person.

This basic understanding of names renders it possible for the Igbo to appropriate the Judaeo-Christian law, which forbids taking the name of God in vain. In some Nigerian cultures, to call someone older by their first name is considered sacrilegious and an uncultured act.[27] Frequently prefixes such as *daa* or *dede*, auntie or uncle function as a hedge that secures the aura of the first name of an older person. Examples include *daa Nwaobira*, auntie Mercy or *dede Amacha*, where the named is older than then user. Persons who are of approximately close in age address

---

26. Tarr, *Double Image*, 159.
27. Oyewumi, "(Re) constituting the Cosmology," 107.

each other by their first names. Oftentimes the name of a child serves in identifying its mother or father such as mama *Uwanaghiakwa* or papa *Chinedu*. The underscoring depths of significance in a name enable one to begin to unravel its metaphoric connotation.

Given the connotation of a name in Igbo culture, naming a child becomes a conscious and attentive act. A child unfairly named carries a life-long burden. In Genesis 35:16–19, for example, dying Rachel names her second born son, *Ben-oni*, meaning son of my affliction. Jacob aware of the gravity of the name *Ben-oni* and the burden it evokes quickly renames the infant, *Ben-ja-min*, meaning son of my right hand. One may add that the child born to the widow of Phinehas after Israel lost the Ark to the Philistines was named, Ichabod "Gone is the glory from Israel" (I Sam 4: 19–22).

The burden an unfair name sustains bears on indignity and a sense of loss. Nigerian scholar Chimalum Nwankwo echoed the Igbo attitude towards derogatory names stating that "In Igbo culture, to give or call one a name which one does not like and accept is another ultimate insult."[28] The conclusion suggests that derogatory female names symbolize the ultimate disrespect for the female human being. One so poorly named is bereft of hope and basic creativity that a name fosters. A pejoratively named person sinks into a kind of poverty, a poverty that extends beyond physical. This kind of poverty strikes at the very essence of one's being as well as that of the society where the collective well-being derives from individual flourishing.[29] Denigrating names negate Bujo's compelling argument that the individual can enrich the community only when she/he is made a person by its individual members.[30] This religious anthropology persuades contemporary African theologians to insist that the abundant life remains the goal of African theology. These theologians must also recognize that the affirmation of abundance (Exod 16:17–18; John 10:10), rooted in the generosity of God, is profoundly subversive to the deeply dominant version of reality.[31] Had theologians recognized the gravity of the call to abundant life, women in Africa would be integrated fully into social processes.

28. Nwankwo, "The Lake Goddess: The Roots of Nwapa's Word," 338.
29. Oduyoye, *Introducing*, 34.
30. Bujo, *Foundations of an African Ethic*, 93.
31. Brueggemann, *Word Militant*, 153.

The question becomes how does one characterize the abundant life when society gives some of her members' names that represent life-denying prospects? Does such naming not conceal a destructive judgment that diminishes the idea of human flourishing and as such makes community and communion ineffectual? If the purpose of existence consists in community and communion, what reading can render liberative, such pejorative female names as *Nwanyibuife* (*Nwa-nyi-bu-ife*), *Nwanwanyikwa*, (short form *Nwanyikwa*,), *Nwa-nyi-kwa*), and *Ejinwanwanyiemenini* (short form *Ejinwanyiemenini*), *Eji-nwa-nwa-nyi-eme-ni-ni*), which can be translated respectively as "a female is also something," "a female child again," and "what can one do with a female"? These names are not merely a convenient collocation of sounds by which a person could be identified. They represent a marker, which suggests ideologies of subordination and marginalization. Perhaps one can find an ally in responding to the negative effects these names evoke in the oracle of Jeremiah 1:10 and possibly Nehemiah, 2:18, one which insists on rooting out, tearing down, destroying and reconstructing.[32] While employing this hermeneutics of reconstruction, a "hermeneutics of suspicion" will also enable the seeking out of social interests that shaped name texts that foster sexism, marginalization and other forms of oppression against women. Insights drawn from these analyses provide the tools with which to investigate and reconstruct debasing female names. The character of Beatrice Nwanyibuife in *Anthills of the Savannah* serves as a starting point of the conversation.

The choice of *Anthills* relates to the theme of redemption subtly imaged by the female characters in the novel. The redemptive idea is consistent with the role of biblical *doulas*, heroic women who mediate God's saving power in Israel. Pertinent issues in the narrative resonate with biblical, ethical, and cultural themes that I grapple with in making a contribution to reimaging and constructing a positive image of women. Following Nehemiah's injunction, "Let us begin to rebuild."

---

32. Brueggemann, *Word Militant*, 14–16. See, also Dedji, *Reconstruction and Renewal*, 2.

NAME AND NAMING: DECONSTRUCTION AND RECONSTRUCTION

Anthills of the Savannah

Achebe locates *Anthills* in the context of religion and culture, particularly that of the Nigeria, of which Igbo ethos emerges. In *Anthills*, Achebe tells a story of three schoolmates and friends, Sam, Chris, and Ikem, who became major figures in a new regime in Kanga, a fictional nation of West Africa. The author addresses the course unbridled power often takes and demonstrates how the fierce pursuit of self-interest comes at a tremendous cost to the community as a whole. Consequently, the three friends paid the ultimate price because they forgot that "this world belongs to the people of the world not to any little caucus, no matter how talented."[33]

Significantly, the author creates fully developed female characters in the novel and suggests that the women remain sources of moral strength, tradition, and hope in the face of violence and deception. Friendly to all three men, Beatrice Nwanyibuife, the chief protagonist, attempts to temper the strident masculinity of the Kanga society with the feminine principles of love, peace, and nurture. She attempts to rebuild and heal the society devastated by male aggression and abuse of power.[34] In this story of death and devastation, Beatrice Nwanyibuife broke the deadlock of the conflict situation. Becoming the leader of the remnant, she is a type of *doulē kyriou*, and the progenitor of a new society.

Beatrice Nwanyibuife

In *Anthills*, the author grounds gender in the character of the female protagonist, Beatrice Nwanyibuife. He reflects modernity and Igbo tradition in the hybridity of Western and Igbo names: Beatrice Nwanyibuife. The emerging new social order in which the female plays a key role announces the future of the reconstructed Kanga symbolized by the name given to a girl-child, *Amaechina* (*ama-echi-na*), meaning, may-the-path-never-close. Born to Elewa, a simple uneducated woman and a girlfriend of the slain Ikem, *Amaechina* would become a symbol in the new Kanga. Significantly, three females: Beatrice Nwanyibuife, Elewa

---

33. Muoneke, *Art, Rebellion and Redemption*, 152.
34. Schreiters, *Ministry of Reconciliation*, 152.

and Amaechina take over the story of Kanga replacing the three males: Sam, Chris, and Ikem who brought death and destruction to the old Kanga. The women, like Israel's *doulas*, savior figures, were left to carry on the society. Under the leadership of Beatrice Nwanyibuife, the remnants of Kanga form a micro-society from which new life rose, that new life is represented by Amaechina.

Achebe represents the dual name Beatrice Nwanyibuife as a metaphoric text. The name Beatrice Nwanyibuife can represent concomitantly the most debilitating and most invigorating trajectories of the life of a female in Igbo society.

Metaphorically, the dual name represents several possibilities. At one level, the name contrasts Igbo tradition with Christianity and shows how one can redeem the other. While the name Beatrice represents Christianity, Nwanyibuife stands for the Igbo cultural context. At another level, the names seem to deal with the question of the restoration of women in post-colonial context. The context of restoration integrates the Igbo past, present, and future. Achebe blends these epochs in the activities of the central female character, Beatrice Nwanyibuife, an unmarried and Western-educated public servant. This character, who serves, becomes a source of passion and inspiration in the narrative, because to serve is to reign. She symbolizes the fundamental quality of the female, the one who leads the community. Not only peculiar to the Igbo, the Akan of Ghana celebrates women's leadership role in community. An Akan proverb reinforces women's leadership role by noting that most Akan migration stories place women at the center, with women leading the community to freedom and prosperity.[35]

In this story, Beatrice Nwanyibuife is born into a Christian family. Her father Okoh is a Christian school teacher and her mother presumably is a homemaker. The family succumbs to patriarchal ethos that places less value on the girl-child by giving their fifth daughter the name Nwanyibuife – a female is also something. Later in life, the character of Beatrice Nwanyibuife reminiscences:

> I did not realize until much later that my mother bore me a huge grudge because I was a girl—her fifth in a row though one had died—and that when I was born she had so desperately prayed for a boy to give my father. This knowledge came to me by slow stages which I won't go into now. But I must mention that in addi-

---

35. Oduyoye, *Daughters of Anowa*, 8.

tion to Beatrice they had given me another name at my baptism, Nwanyibuife – A female is also something. Can you beat that? Even as a child I disliked the name most intensely without being aware of its real meaning . . . it seemed fudged![36]

Evidently, the giving of such a pejorative name in the context of baptism suggests an ironic situation. On face value, the name makes a judgment on the liberative teaching of the Gospel. The undercurrent in the scenario, however, represents the imaginative field of patriarchy, with all its epistemological assumptions and socio-cultural exhibits of hegemony, placing the female as the "other," that which "is also something."

Nwanyibuife instinctively senses the burden her given name conveys. She disliked the name most intensely as a child even without understanding its full significance. In an inchoate manner, she understood the name Nwanyibuife as a construction that suppresses her female embodiment. She rejects it because in her imagination, she senses an alternative to what the name signifies. The denunciation of the name points to another possibility. This girl-child intuits that another world for the female remains a possibility, because the world she presently inhabits does not represent a given. It represents a fraud, something "fudged", a distortion, a scheme designed to skew the veracity of the female.

This female's prophetic self was manifest even as a child; she listened and imagined differently. She entertained different realities in her "other world," *uwa-t-uwa* where deep calls on deep. Her *uwa-t-uwa*, meaning "world inside a world inside a world without end," became the root metaphor, the tap root that nourished her imagination of an "alternative community." In her thought, the name Nwanyibuife did not account for the dignity she possessed as a female. She instinctively recognizes the burden that the name signifies and summarily rejects it.

Regrettably, the naming of the protagonist Nwanyibuife empties the field of the possible action by God (*Chukwunaenyinwa*, God is the giver of offspring). A name such as Nwanyibuife suggests that humans assume to run the world by their own idiom, disregarding the Igbo religious traditions that privileges the Providential order of existence. Thus redemption of the female who "is also something" seems to lie in the Christian name Beatrice.

The juxtaposing of a Christian and an Igbo traditional name within the context of a baptism is highly symbolic. Like most symbols, what the

36. Achebe, *Anthills*, 86–87.

name does not say provides a clue to what it belies. Although in the narrative, Nwanyibuife functions figuratively in the place of its literal meaning, the name still raises a fundamental question about female identity. What does a female-child represent in the community? Without doubt, the circumstances surrounding this child's birth, "the fifth girl in a row," suggest an ambivalent response.

Literally, Nwanyibuife, "a female is also something," conjures up an alternative choice. Any person of Igbo origin hearing the name Nwanyibuife, would at once recognize its implication, that the naming family would rather have a male child in place of the female, that the family has one girl too many! This passion for a male offspring represents a benchmark of patrilineal society. The society believes that a continuation of the family remains connected with a male progeny. Thus, the absence of sons represents the worst kind of misfortune that can befall a family.

The obsession with a male progeny among the Igbo, however, may point to another direction. It reveals a deeper concern residing in the Igbo non-Christian past, the cult of the living-dead or ancestors.[37] Because the warp and woof of Igbo existence revolve around constant recall of the presence of their living-dead, a public function, that they reserved for their male, it becomes imperative to have a male-child to fulfill this role. Similar circumstances exist even in societies considered matrilineal. The Nigerian Scholar, Amakievi Gabriel observes the phenomenon among some Ijoid and Delta-Edoid communities in Nigeria. Gabriel states "In the matrilineal communities, descent is traced through the female line but the oldest male (not female) heads the lineage and performs political and religious functions on behalf of the lineage."[38]

In Igbo thought, the living-dead represent the concentration of life and vital energy necessary for the birth of all members of the lineage. A conscious, as well as an unconscious, awareness of the "cult" of the living-dead implicitly informs the Igbo attitude towards progeny. Mbiti comments on the link between children and the living-dead as having roots in the African concept of personal immortality:

---

37. Ilogu, *Christianity in Ibo Culture*, 130." See, also Jean-Marc Éla, *My Faith as an African*, 16, 14.

38. Gabriel, "The Dynamics of Culture and Feminism among the Izon and the Edo of the Niger Delta," 40.

> This concept of personal immortality should help us to understand the religious significance of marriage in African societies. Unless a person has close relatives to remember him when he has physically died, then he is nobody and simply vanishes out of human existence like a flame when it is extinguished. It remains a duty, religious and ontological, for everyone to get married; and if a man has no children or only daughters, he finds another wife so that through her, children (or sons) may be born who would survive him and keep him (with the other living-dead of the family) in personal immortality.[39]

Without a family cult of the living-dead, the link between the living and living-dead ceases. Dead relatives remain eternally dead with no prospects for the afterlife. Such a scenario destroys the tripartite notion of community, which consists of the living, the yet to be born, and the living-dead. An unbroken link guarantees a participation in the fullness of life that goes beyond physical existence.[40]

Even Beatrice Nwanyibuife's Christian family was not immune from this deep-seated cultural belief. Hence, Beatrice Nwanyibuife's mother bore her "a huge grudge," because her birth disappointed the family's hope for immortality. Accordingly, the name Nwanyibuife unequivocally registers the family's deepest disappointment. Nwanyibuife, even as a child, deciphers the textual element of her given name as inimical to her *being*, and hence detests the "fudged" name. This sense of rejection of that which "seemed fudged," is emblematic of the stand women must take against cultural norms they consider oppressive. Like a typical metaphor, the literal meaning of the dual names comprises two contradictory terms. While Nwanyibuife suggests a female's reduced status, the name Beatrice offers a more positive image.

The name Beatrice derives from the Latin name *Beatrix*, meaning she who makes people happy, the one who brings happiness to the group. Beatrice also means "voyager through blessed life."[41] Metaphorically, the name Beatrice reveals that the female character symbolizes a light, a blessing. Beatrice signifies a verity spoken of as "something" that renews the community. Pope Benedict XVI would describe that something as "not just something, but somebody [*Nwanyi*, a female], capable of

---

39. Mbiti, *African Religions and Philosophy*, 25.
40. Mbiti, *African Religions and Philosophy*, 141.
41. Room, *Dictionary of First Names*, 91–92.

self-knowledge, self-possession, free self-giving, and entering into communion with others."[42] This understanding of the female as "somebody" is consistent with the character of the biblical *doulē* (Luke 1:38), the servant of the LORD. In like manner, reinterpreting Nwanyibuife can yield analogous meaning.

Igbo tonal language offers the possibility of a subversive reading of the name Nwanyibuife. Dividing the name Nwanyibuife into three/four syllabi yields: (1) *Nwa-nyi* (2) *bu* (3) *ife*. While the first syllable "*Nwa-nyi*" translates *female*, the second, "*bu*," represents the to-be verb, *is*. The shift occurs in the last syllable, *ife*. *Ife* can translate into *something*, as in the text or into *light*. Thus the reinterpreted meaning of Nwanyibuife can read "female-is-light." This redeemed interpretation of the name Nwanyibuife represents a deeper meaning of the metaphor, which the dominant interpretation name-text hardly expresses. Possibly, the luminous qualities of the female remain concealed behind "something." Perchance the "also something" which conceals female luminous qualities, represents what Pope Benedict XVI terms "capability for self-knowledge."

The subverted or redeemed meaning of *Nwanyibuife*, "female is light," when yoked with Beatrice, "bringer of joy, the one who blesses," yields a fuller picture of the Igbo female identity: female, bringer of joyful light or a bearer of luminous blessings. This symbolism of joyful light is significant in interpreting the *doulē kyriou*. Equally significant is the idea of remnant in *Anthills*. These themes closely parallel Matthew's presentation of Mary in his narrative of Jesus' genealogy. Latina theologians Ivone Gebara and María Clara Bingemer, highlight Mary's luminous joyful quality stating "The woman is the symbol of the faithful people [remnant], from whom the Messiah is born . . . the light-filled face of the people, God's faithfulness constantly reemerging from the ruins of destruction." [43] One can make a similar claim about all the women in Matthew's genealogy of Jesus. In the thick of a patriarchal account of Jesus genealogy, Matthew clearly demonstrates that God employs women's luminosity in saving God's people: Tamar, Rahab, Ruth, the wife of Uriah, and Mary (cf. Matt 1:2–16).

This subverted reading of the name Beatrice Nwanyibuife comes close to Dante's Beatrice. Nigerian scholar Romanus Muoneke contends

---

42. Pope Benedict XVI, 2007 World Day of Peace Message.
43. Gebara and Bingemer, "Mary," 168.

that the characters of Beatrice Nwanyibuife and Dante's Beatrice represent redemptive figures: "In Dante's *Divine Comedy*, Beatrice signifies divine revelation. It is Beatrice who guides Dante through Earthly Paradise, whereby brotherly love and humility reign to the celestial realm, where the dominant image is that of light. In *Anthills*, Beatrice plays a similar role by fostering the new spirit of love and humility in micro-society. She guides the group through the dark tunnel of events to the light of understanding."[44] The theme of light in the names underscores the specificity of the female. In a progressive weaving manner, *Anthills* employs various strands of female characteristics to make the point.

Juxtaposing the baptism name, Beatrice Nwanyibuife, expresses a single complex idea of what it means to be a female in a Christianized Igbo society. The hybridity of name, Beatrice Nwanyibuife, conjures up at once always Igbo and always striving to be Christian. This scenario produces a bifurcation of consciousness, each consciousness speaking to the other. The symbol, Beatrice Nwanyibuife, a "daughter of Idemili," the Goddess of the waters, and a Christian represents the link between Igbo traditional past and its Westernized present. In this sense, the dual name constitutes more than emotive value because it offers new information about female reality. The dual names explain why most Igbo Christians have two names, one native the other foreign. Early evangelizers did not recognize that name texts represent important cultural markers. Or perhaps, the contention on relegating the native names was part of effacing the indigenous culture that was then considered pagan. The name, Beatrice, however, advances a liberative meld that represents the core of the resolution of women's identity in contemporary Igbo society.

In addition, this ability to interpret provides the key that unlocks and liberates texts inimical to women. The American scholar Vincent L. Wimbush forcefully states that the ability to interpret shows that one is fully human. The truly free individual represents one who seeks meaning through reading, "radical reading—open-ended readings about the self in the world, necessarily including the past readings that represent openness to other ways of knowing that expand the boundaries."[45] The character of Beatrice Nwanyibuife, evidently radically, read her double name, which she appropriated and embodied. She demonstrated her

---

44. Muoneke, *Art, Rebellion and Redemption*, 152.
45. Wimbush, "Signifying on Scriptures," 256.

role as the happy light shining on the remnant, the custodian of the community's core values: peace, love and justice.

In *Anthills*, therefore, an imaginative creativity coalesces with passion to produce that which women can appropriate for self-identification. Thus, the "light" emanating from *Beatrice* metaphorically shines on that which "seemed fudged," *Nwanyibuife*, exposing its true meaning, two brilliant lights adjacent to each other. The Beatrice metaphor within the framework of *Anthills* continues to unravel when placed within the larger context of African women in modern history, particularly in the context of the Beatrice of the Congo. Achebe's Beatrice in *Anthills* is reminiscent of this historic Congolese seventeenth-century prophetess.

Kimpa Vita (c. 1682—1706), Beatrice of the Congo

The symbolic name, Beatrice, has a prized place in African's modern history. Born, Kimpa Vita (c. 1682—1706), this young woman of noble birth received the name Beatrice at baptism. Dona Beatrice is one of the best-known women religious figures in modern Africa.[46] Beatrice of the Congo rose to prominence when she felt the ruins of her country and called for the restoration of political order through religious regeneration. She formed an African Movement inspired by biblical teachings. Believing herself possessed by the spirit of St. Anthony of Padua, Beatrice named her group of followers after the Saint. Seen as a mystic of renowned integrity, Beatrice's religio-political involvement drew strong support among peasants. In the climate of the day the Antonian Movement was declared a heretical sect and persecution ensued. At the instigation of the Italian Capuchin missionaries, Beatrice Kimpa Vita was condemned as a heretic. Both she and her infant son were burned at the stake as heretics in 1706 and her Movement disbanded. However, the spirit of the Movement continued to survive underground for more than two centuries. A trace of Beatrice's vision rooted in African symbolism marks African Indigenous Churches (AIC).[47] In some AIC women participate in the highest leadership and ministerial roles. The AIC remain self-sufficient and self ministering; never receiving support from outside the continent. A striking similarity appears between Kimpa Vita and Joan of Arc, a fifteenth century national heroine of France. Both young,

---

46. Coquery-Vidrovitch, *African Women*, 47.

47. Duncan & Kalu, "Bakuzufu: Revivial Movements and Indigenous Appropriation in African Christianity," 267.

imaginative women had great passion for their people. The active role of this Congolese light bearer in Church and society no longer can be ignored by mainline Christian churches. The attempt of Beatrice, "the bearer of light," to indigenize the biblical teachings in her native Congo more than three centuries ago, draws attention to materials that can be retrieved in the reconstruction of the image of women in contemporary Africa.

Beatrice Nwanyibuife and Amaechina

As a rhetorical figure, the name Beatrice Nwanyibuife represents other levels of interpretation. A victim of patriarchal subordination and one who bore the burden of a name not her own, Beatrice Nwanyibuife did not play the victim. The oppressive milieu in which she found herself propelled her to prove that a female can indeed become somebody rather than be merely "also something." She can indeed become somebody, a *doulē*, one who renews and revitalized the community. The story of Israel's matriarchs and that of the Lukan *doulē* suggest no less. Thus the character of Beatrice Nwanyibuife challenges patriarchal structures represented by the leadership of Sam, Chris, and Ikem as well as the "male chauvinism" she experienced in her father's house.[48] In the end, Beatrice Nwanyibuife became that someone who offers Kanga hope that ushers in a new beginning, a new reality for a devastated people.

This new reality is symbolized in the birth of a girl-child. In naming the child, Beatrice Nwanyibuife echoes an Old Testament prophet and declares, "we have our own version of hope that springs eternal." We shall call this child AMAECHINA: May-the-path-never-close.[49] Amaechina (ama-echi-na) is a typical and an exclusively male name. Born to Elewa, a simple semi-literate woman and posthumously to Ikem, one of Kanga's trios, (the other two being Sam and Chris), Amaechina would be different. Naming a girl-child an exclusively male name portends newness, a symbol of continuity in the new society. In so naming, Achebe institutes a new era for women in the society.

Achebe makes a momentous assertion in his representation of the three significant female characters: Nwanyibuife, Elewa, and Amaechina as the cornerstone of the new society. His depiction of these female char-

---

48. Achebe, *Anthills*, 88.
49. Achebe, *Anthills*, 222.

acters bears family resemblance to the story of Ruth and Naomi in the Hebrew Bible and more so to Mary and Elizabeth in the births narratives in Luke's Gospel (Luke 1). The literary critic, Achebe, is not unlike biblical authors in his contrasting the female with the male in relation to securing the future of society. In *Anthills*, the three women (Nwanyibuife, Elewa, and Amaechina), replace the old society, which stood on three male characters: Sam, Chris, and Ikem. The latter brought death and destruction to the old Kanga. The former brought hope and redemption. That hope is crystallized in may-the-path-never-close, Amaechina.

It seems to me that Achebe fashioned most of his female characters in *Anthills* from the pages of the Bible. A close parallel exists in the naming of Amaechina and Obed in the Book of Ruth. Two women, Ruth and Naomi "gave birth" to a male child, Obed. In a similar manner, Beatrice Nwanyibuife and Elewa, the girlfriend of fallen Ikem, "gave birth" to a female child, named Amaechina, a girl with a symbolic male name. In *Anthills*, the remnant of Kanga names the newborn. In the Book of Ruth, the women of a Bethlehem neighborhood name a son born to Boaz and Ruth, Obed. The American biblical scholar, Carol Myers, comments on the Ruth episode: "That a group of women names the child is unusual, as is also the implication that both Ruth and Naomi are mothers of the infant. Usually mothers, but sometimes fathers, bestow names on newborns. Having two mothers and a whole group of female name-givers perhaps signifies Obed's role as progenitor of the future dynastic founder, who will belong to a whole nation."[50] Like Obed, Amaechina literally had two mothers: Elewa and Beatrice Nwanyibuife. By proposing, a traditionally male name for a girl-child, the author puts the girl-child on equal footing with the male as progenitor of the future society. In another sense, Amaechina represents the Pentecost era. The name echoes Luke's writings on the Pentecost in the Acts of the Apostles. Peter quotes the prophet Joel to declare the age as when God's *doulos* and *doulas* (sons and daughters) shared equally in the new life of the Spirit (Acts 2: 17–21). The metaphoric significance of Amaechina represents the desired future of Kanga. Generally, the privilege of naming a new born in the culture in which *Anthills* is cast devolves on an elder who is usually a male. But this right became also the duty of a young female, Beatrice Nwanyibuife. She suggests a name and invites the group to name the child. The singular act of communal naming symbolically

---

50. Achebe, *Anthills*, 254.

indicates the active participation and engagement of each member of the new society in reconstructing and recreating a community mirrored in the name, may-the-path-never-close. It suggests the flourishing together that guarantees the fullness of life for the community. Specifically, the community's involvement in the naming reiterates the ethos that maintaining the commonweal is not the preserve of a single individual. Neither is sustaining the community reserved to a group of friends no matter how intelligent, nor does it dependent on patriarchal structures. Upholding the good of the community remains the right as well as the duty of the entire community, women as well as men, an act of solidarity, which the naming of Amaechina symbolizes. The naming of the new born reveals yet, another aspect of the metaphor of Beatrice Nwanyibuife. She represents the new woman who challenges tradition in its incapacitating aspects. Although not a mother, and still unmarried, Beatrice Nwanyibuife possesses the power of naming and forges a future characterized by relationality and solidarity. Thus, this female character becomes a beacon of hope for the micro-society that survives Kanga's devastation. The activity of the group in itself stimulates a sense of restoration. Such communal undertaking reawakens the spirit of communal living, the very essence of most African traditional communal identity. Besides the group's activity rekindles the "we-ethos," the "we-logic" by which traditional societies understood themselves.

Not unlike Israel's *doulas* Beatrice Nwanyibuife demonstrates great scope and confidence in her ability to deal with ambiguous situations. Like biblical Abigail, Beatrice Nwanyibuife shows understanding, good judgment, and decides as well as acts wisely in life threatening circumstances. Similar to biblical Esther, she invites herself into the area that her gender forbade her (cf. Esth Add B 4:11; Add D). Literally, this female protagonist takes up the will to arise. A liberative aspect of the *Anthills* narrative consists in the challenge it offers to traditions unfavorable to women's integral wellbeing. The metaphor of Beatrice Nwanyibuife represents the new woman who challenges tradition in its incapacitating aspects. She survives to tell the story of what was Kanga, and to become the remnant leader. Reflections on two real and contemporary female names in the next section will substantiate and confirm the various ways the ideology of subordination remains entrenched in certain female names.

Reflection on Contemporary Female Names

The focus on gender, a dominant factor in Igbo life, creates ambiguity by the use of some traditional female names. There are extant female names which appear pejorative, undignified, inane, degrading, and unjust. Degrading female names represent a subtle form of silencing and as such have a potential for violence. A pejorative name minimizes the bearer's presence and creates a seemingly impenetrable barrier. The menacing aspect of unjust names reminds one that those so named, even if conscious of its deeper meaning, often appear powerless to change the name because of massive cultural constructions designed to maintain the status quo. The inability to act, however, does not suggest acquiescence. In *Anthills*, Nwanyibuife, even as a child, disliked her given "name most intensely" but she could not change it. She, however, retired into her *uwa-t-uwa* where she nurtured an imagination for later engagement with life.

Significantly, only women in Igbo society have names that can be considered offensive. The sustained practice makes such names problematic. Examples of some names reveal how Igbo society sustains the image of women as the "other": *Nwanyibuego/ Nwanyibuaku*, (*nwanyi* = female, *bu* = is, *ego/aku* = money/wealth), "a female is money/wealth"; *Ejinwanyiemenini*, "what can one do with a female /of what use is a female child?" Another version of the name is *Nwanyimeole* (*Nwa-nyi-me-ole*), "what can a female do?" *Nwanyikwa*, "a female child again!" *Amandem*, "lineage of females!" *Amandem* clearly states that there are no males in the family. The name *Amandem* appears as a "death sentence." A girl so named in many instances, is not allowed to marry. She is made to remain in the family and raise children, sons, of cause, for the son-less father! Interview subjects insist that generally women are given flattering or apologetic names. Flattery names such as *Nwanyinna*, "daddy's girl"; *Nwaobira/Obiagaeli*, "the one who has come to enjoy good fortunes"; *Nwaugo*, "the one as beautiful as an eagle," represent common examples. Even such names as *Chinyere* or *Chinyerenwa* (a child is a gift from God) and *Nkechinyere* are not innocent. The latter in particular speaks of resignation. The prefix: *Nke*, gives its meaning away. It suggests "the one," which in context can read, "I take that which I have been given although I would have preferred to have been given a male child." *Nwanyibuife*, *Nwanyikwa*, *Ejinwanyiemeni* represent the other end of the spectrum.

The wide range of names indicates that the polemics employed to construct women range from subtle to severe. Besides some female praise names, particularly that of married women, equally can conceal language of subordination. Such include *Odozi aku*, "the one who takes care of possessions/wealth," or *Ori aku*, "the one who enjoys the wealth." Such praise names within nuptials relations, undermine the covenantal understanding of marriage, and place the female outside the covenant presenting her as a mere custodian in her matrimonial home. She represents but a steward to guard the accumulated possessions "to keep a close watch on the income, to take charge of the household."[51] By accepting the encomium, *odozi aku*, women implicate themselves in their own subjugation. Name change in marriage has similar effect. Oduyoye notes that name change in marriage represents the civil death of women. Such name change makes subordination under the law possible. Oduyoye further states that by law, couples may choose a new name. No law authorizes adopting the name of the groom.[52] Before the advent of westernization, however, women in Igbo society never change names at marriage. Married women keep their maiden names. The Senegalese historian, anthropologist, physicist, and politician, *Cheikh Anta Diop* stated that in many African societies, the wife kept her totem, meaning her domestic god, therefore, retained her natural family name, her legal identity, after marriage.[53] Cultural underpinnings as these mitigated the gender divide. But name continue to provide the weapon for the covert gender battle. Names suggestive of objectification, inconsequentiality, and of ephemeral significance burden the bearer in a subtle way, and not only the bearer for a single pejoratively-named female dehumanizes all females. A reflection the names *Nwanyikwa* and *Ejinwanyiemenini* underscore the characterization of the female as the "other" and provide a quintessential example of construction by deconstruction. Engaging these names exposes the true identity of the female buried under a layer of false identity. Such engagement reveals what Siker insightfully articulates as "a depth identity behind a surface identity."[54]

---

51. Okure, "Women in the Bible," 50.

52. Personal conversation with Mercy Amba Oduyoye, at the University of San Francisco, October 3, 2007.

53. Cheikh Anta Diop, *Civilization or Barbariam*, 112.

54. Siker, "Unmasking the Enemy," 122.

Nwanyikwa

The name Nwanyikwa literally means "a female again!" Actually, *Nwanyikwa* represents an abridged form of either Nwanyiozokwa, or Nwanyikeekwa, or Nwanyiozokeekwa, which means "another female child again!"

Nwanwanyikwa: The prefix, *nwa* - translates offspring. *Nwanyi* therefore, means female offspring. The suffix, *-kwa* could translate "again," and in which case is synonymous with *ozo* or *ozokeekwa -Kwa* can equally mean "also," "too" or "again."

The context of the name Nwanyikwa, "a female child again?" is closely related to that of Nwanyibuife "a female is also something." Nwanyikwa reads disappointment. The name alerts the reader that the naming family's yearning for a male-offspring remains unfulfilled because female children keep coming in succession. Such unfulfilled desires can be a source of marital or familial problems. Some persons ignorantly believe that the female partner is solely responsible in determining the gender of the child. Some men take on, or sometimes are persuaded by families to take on, a concubine or a second wife to bear a son to their name. The Igbo experience is not an isolated occurrence. Henry VII is an example of a similar experience in the England of his time. It is common historical knowledge that the main reason Henry VIII broke away from the Roman Catholic Church was to father a son to continue the dynasty. Since Rome would not grant him a divorce from Catherine Aragon, who failed to produce a male heir. King Henry broke away, divorced Catherine and married Anne Boyleyn. But the story did not end there. Eventually, the Tudor dynasty continued without a male heir, a female, Mary I, the only surviving daughter of Catherine of Aragon became England's fourth crowned monarch. But these happened some five hundred years ago. The Igbo experience, however, represents a contemporary example.

Strangely enough, in an Igbo family household, having a number of male children in a row is never a problem. There can never be too many males. The next male child in a row of males can never be given the name *Nwanwokokwa* "a male child again!" The designation *Nwanwokokwa*, the opposite of *Nwanwanyikwa* is inconceivable in the Igbo imagination.

The drama of female name climaxes at the birth of a male-child after a row of female children. The name of the new arrival reveals the full import of the Igbo valuation of the female embodied in pejorative names. This male-child is given a name(s) that reflects flourishing, stability, valor, prosperity, and continuity. The child receives names such as *Chukwuemeka*, "The Supreme Deity has done well"; *Obilor*, "may my heart/soul have its rest"; *Ahamefula*, "may-my name-never-be lost or cease to be." *Amaechina/Uzuechina/Obiechina*, "may-the-path-never-close." These exclusively male names suggest that the offspring which came before them, which often are girls, do not count. Why names, such as *Chukwuemeka* that panegyrize the Almighty, cannot be given to a female raises a red flag.

In actual fact, *Nwanyikwa* "another female child again?" does not represent a real name in the sense that the Igbo understand name. Rather *Nwanyikwa* depicts an *empty* name devoid of a personality. Empty naming does not exclude turning the girl-child into a faceless, voiceless, valueless human being because the very language of naming socializes. If a name corresponds to the unique personality of a child, naming a child *Nwanyikwa*, does not carry any aura of uniqueness. Such a name tends to symbolize "nonentity." Moreover, since a name sometimes corresponds to the identity of a person, a person given a pejorative name is deprived of a model of self-identification. Thus a denial of identity translates into exclusion from participation in social processes.

The backdrop to such name as *Nwanyiozokeekwa* is connected to inheritance rights and the cult of the ancestors. Women generally do not have inheritance rights in a "thick" patriarchal society. In a patrilineal society, inheritance exists through the male line. Biblically that was not the case at the formation of the tribes in ancient Israel. A critical reading of the Book of Numbers on "Property of Heiresses," reveals that women had inheritance (36:1–12). The context represents the beginning of the formation of the tribe of Israel. Zelophechad, from the tribe of Manasseh, gave his five daughters, Mahlah, Tirzah, Hoglah, Milcah and Noah inheritance alongside their male counterparts. Evidently, Zelophechad, had no difficulty with this arrangement. The settlement, however, became a source of concern after his death. After his death, Zelophechad's clansmen sought to reverse his will (Num 36:1). In the verses that followed, Moses gave partial judgment to the clansmen but not without injury to the women. The law subjected the women to marry within their own clan so as to keep their inheritance in the family. Curiously, the women retained their inheritance. Moses' verdict suggests that had the women chosen to remain unmarried, the issue of female inheritance would not have arisen.

This case represents another construction of women and the structures that burden women. The discussion bears on Jesus' discourse on divorce in Mark 10:1–12. In the Matthean text, marriage was established as a permanent commitment of both spouses *in the beginning*. The "hardness of [men's] heart," however, forced Moses to institute the divorce ordinance. In the Book of Numbers inheritance case, the hardness of the heart of Zelophechad's clansmen again forced Moses to enact an ordinance concerning inheritance of heiresses.

Significantly, the third to last verse of the Book of Job deals with inheritance. Job gave his three daughters, Jemimah, Keziah, and Kerenhappuch inheritance with their brethren (Job 42:13–15). Persuasively, Scripture records the names of the women whose fathers extended inheritance rights. Name recognition also exposes the assertion that women in this society "were not counted."

Nigerian Ify Amadiume, Ghanaian Oduyoye, and Catherine Coquery-Vidrovitch, among other scholars describe how some African families resolve the issue of inheritance. These scholars identify a phenomenon where a female child can become "woman-man," or male daughters" among the Igbo or "house daughters among the Ibibios." When the survival of the lineage was imperiled by lack of a male heir, a daughter might be turned into a 'woman-man' to head the household until a son could take over from her.[55] The cultural scenario contravenes the image of daughter portrayed in the Book of Sirach, "And the birth of a daughter is a loss" (Sir 22:3). These arrangements demonstrate how "thin" patrifocal interpretations can become in some African societies.

The modest value attached to a female child sometime corresponds to her social worth. Names such as *Nwanyibuego/Nwanyibuaku*, "a female is wealth," embody female social significance. As rhetorical figure, *Nwanyibuego* represents an objectification of the female *par excellence*. In the market economy, the girl-child represents a source of wealth. At marriage, she attracts a bride-wealth. Bride-wealth can, but not necessarily, add value to her parent's economic status because the bride was not bartered. In a sense, she is on loan to the groom because at death, her remains are interred with her ancestors in her natal home. However, the

---

55. Oduyoye, *Daughters of Anowa*, 80. See also Amadiume, *Male Daughters, Female Husbands*, Coquery-Vidrovitch, *African Women*, 55.

bride represents a source of work and a guarantee of children. Father's may use their daughters to advance socially or politically. Saul, for example uses his daughter Michal, to seal a political alliance with David (cf. 1 Sam 18:27). Daughters in Igbo society provide a secured insurance against old age. Even in contemporary times, it is not uncommon for women in Igbo society who have only male children to intensely desire a girl-child because the female children tend to be more likely than the male to care for aged parents.

Regardless of patriarchal oppressive structures women persistently seek a positive form of identification to enable them to participate and flourish within the community. Identity constitutes essentially a matter of self-perception. When naming denies a girl-child a sense of self, it robs her of a model of positive self-identification. Her capability of perceiving the world becomes problematic. Consequently, this individual remains a nonentity. The nonentity status of the subject fosters inferiority and "otherness."[56] Evidently, the subject is excluded from defining her personal reality and that of the world in which she exists. She subsists outside the human community. For this girl-child, no escape route is available from the *cul-de-sac* where society places her. But there exists an opportunity for an escape. The idea of the fullness of life the Gospel offers and which contemporary African theology celebrates provides that possibility.

The theology of redemption can create a rupture in the system that sustains the notion of the female as the "other," an idea that deprives her of fuller participation in society. The fissure in the system portends a horrific shake up of patriarchal ordered society.[57] The overhaul entails a massive deconstruction or rather remaking of "women," whom Simone de Beauvoir insightfully summed up as "Women and men are made, not born." Beauvoir's statement suggests that social positioning should not be determined by sex.[58] Beauvoir's insight, "Women and men are made, not born," resonates with that of Nigerian philosopher, Ifeanyi A. Menkiti. Menkiti posits that biological function alone does not confer personhood. A lived experience of the person determines personhood.[59] Because the use of a name in Igbo society functions figuratively

---

56. Schüsler Fiorenza, "Breaking the Silence," 169.
57. Alison, *Raising Abel*, 194.
58. De Beauvoir, *Second Sex*, 301.
59. Menkiti, "Person and Community in African Traditional Thought," 158.

its influence on lived experience becomes significant. The influence of names makes imperative a redemptive interpretation of Mary's self-understanding in her assertion as *doulē kyriou*, servant of the LORD, rather than "Handmaid." This use of a positive designation furthers reconstructing women's image.

Female appraisal in Igbo society compares well in many respects to Jewish appreciation of the female. A Jewish novelist, Anzia Yezierska, captures female objectification in her 1925 novel, *Bread Givers*.[60] This novel constitutes one of the authentic and touching testaments of the struggle of Jewish immigrants, especially Jewish women, to find their way in the new world. Because *Bread Givers* brings women's experience into consideration, it represents an autobiographical source from which to reconstruct the past experience of Jewish American women. The story also shows that these women were primarily breadwinners. Yezierska's story clearly gives voice to women's struggle within patriarchal structure, a struggle that cuts across cultural and religious traditions.

Women, the Jewish Experience: Bread Givers

The Igbo metaphor, *Nwanyibuego/Nwanyibuaku*, "female is wealth," rings clear in Yezierska's novel, *Bread Givers*. In *Bread Givers*, Yezierska narrates the story of a Jewish immigrant family's struggle to break out of the ghetto in New York City at the turn of the twentieth century. A complex story of family, religion, poverty, and survival, the title, *Bread Givers*, remains intricately bound with money, wealth, and livelihood. Every female character in the narrative literally slaved to sustain the male and the rest of family. Held in bondage by their father, the women remained the only source of *Bread* for the family. The story in a creative manner exposes the pretentious role of the male/father as *bread winner*. In this familiar tale, the father supports his scholarly ambition in Talmudic study and provides livelihood for the family by bargaining away three of his four daughters to the highest bidder. Sara, the youngest complains bitterly about her father, Smolinsky, moaning, "His heartlessness to Mother, his pitiless driving away Bessie's only chance to love, bargaining way Fania to a gambler and Mashah to a diamond-faker—when they each had the luck to win lovers of their own—all these tyrannies

---

60. Yezierska, *Bread Givers*.

crushed over me . . . "I can't stand it!"⁶¹ Sara rebelled against the identity meted out to her sisters. A struggle ensued between a father of the Old World and a daughter of the New, a daughter who refused to accept the dominant male version of existence.

The resistance that followed was directed toward a father who believed that no girl can live without a father or a husband to look out for her.⁶² Sara dissented against a father who believed that according to the Torah, only through a man has a woman an existence; only through a man can a woman enter Heaven.⁶³ For a time, Sara dreamed and imagined herself out of this world of her father. Like the prophets, Sara dreamed of an "alternative community," where injustice and oppression rooted in biology did not exist. Sara dreamed herself out of the shadows of patriarchal hegemony, which her father represented. Through the instrumentality of education, she succeeded in entering the world she had dreamed and imagined. She found her own life, a life where her dignity as a female was honored, respected, and secured. Yezierska sums Sara's sense of fulfillment as having a "honeymoon with herself."⁶⁴ Sara would return to take care of her father in his old age but on her own terms as a female with agency and voice in the life's processes. In our ongoing discussion, constructions "fudged" in the art of making women rings true in the name *Nwanyibuife*. The "making of women" constitutes a consolidation of control of those whose power to be depends on denial of being to others.

Pejorative female names such as *Nwanyikwa* confirm androcentric linguistic and ideological systems of legitimization that sustain and contribute to women's silencing and invisibility in the Igbo society. *Ejinwanyiemenini* "what can one do with a female?" represents another silencing name text.

Ejinwanyiemenini

The name *Ejinwanyiemenini*? literally means "what can one do with a female?" Actually, *Ejinwanyiemenini*? represents an abridged form of *Ejinwanwanyiemenini*? "what can one do with a female child?" The name

---

61. Yezierska, *Bread Givers*, 135.
62. Yezierska, *Bread Givers*, 137.
63. Yezierska, *Bread Givers*.
64. Yezierska, *Bread Givers*, 237–241.

is often shortens as *Ejinwanyi*. *Ejinwanwanyiemenini*: broken down into syllables the name reads:

Eji—what; *nwa*—offspring/child; *nwanyi*—female; *emenini*—of what use?

The prefix *Eji-* and the suffix *-emenini* constitute a question. *Eji* and *–emenini* literally mean "Of what use is something?" In this case, it means "Of what use is a female child?" or "What can one do with a female?"

The name *Ejinwanyiemenini*, like *Nwanyibuife* and *Nwanyikwa* represents another construct of the female as "the other." In a world of limited resources, certain persons tend to construct an image of themselves largely by constructing who they are not, that "other." It does imply that in Igbo society, patriarchal sexism constructs the male identity by constructing women through names without any defined matrix.[65] The women's struggle to reconstruct the female identity, however, does not necessarily mean the construction or deconstructing of the male identity. Rather, a reconstruction of female identity employed in my narrative aims at deconstructing those constructions that silence women.

The name *Ejinwanyiemenini* reveals the systematic devaluation and repression of women not only in social structures but in deeply embedded ideological constructs. The name remains tied to female devaluation and exploitation. *Ejinwanyiemenini* is suggestive of female rejection. As in previous contexts, the birth of another female defers the family's hope of continuity and immortality. *Ejinwanyiemenini* implies that women have no purchase on the sphere of highest value and greatest worth; they cannot be an ancestor. Where *Nwanyibuife* expresses disappointment, *Ejinwanyiemenini* expresses an outright lament. In the former, the family accepts the girl-child as a "consolation," *also something*, whereas in the latter, the family *cannot find the use* for the child. Thus, the name, *Ejinwanyiemenini* implies a deep sense of grief, an epic-like drama, "of what use is this child?"

The designation *Ejinwanyiemenini* plugs a hole in the Igbo notion of community. The Igbo who pride themselves as having a high sense of communion based on subsidiarity and solidarity can reject "one female too many." The acclaimed sense of community rooted in Igbo notion of a *Chukwu* and *mmadu* stands betrayed when the community cannot find use for another girl-child. As a rhetorical function, the name

---

65. Siker, "Unmasking the Enemy," 114.

Ejinwanyiemenini invites further information about women. It invites a story, women's story. It invites stories that rake up memories and fire up imagination of women's presence and activities in the Igbo society.

Following Ricoeur's famous dictum "no one speaks from nowhere," it takes an insider, to appreciate the nuance that such an innocuous activity as naming can conceal, and how oppressive certain names can become. William C. Spohn citing Hauerwas makes a claim for the insider status: "Hauerwas and many other narrative theologians reply that no one can adequately assess the truth of a world view without participating in a community which embodies that way of life. In the final analysis the truth of a way of life is decided by examples rather than by theoretical arguments."[66] Certain female names mask cultural idioms and myths, which rule women's lives. Because cultural idioms and myths guarantee that a particular understanding of life passes on, it becomes pertinent to establish the efficacy of the idioms for contemporary applications. Given the pervading role of women in traditional Igbo life, the name designation, *Ejinwanwanyiemenini* "what can one do with a female child" becomes polemical. Several writings from the early colonialists in Igboland, historians as well as anthropologists attest to what the female can do in traditional Igbo societies. One example would elucidate the point.

Women in Traditional Igbo Social Life

In most traditional Igbo societies, women establish agency through marriage. Marriage setup affords women greater latitude for building capacity than men. The practice of exogamous marriage provides women a broader base of interaction with the society than their male counterparts. Normally in this society, the men usually remain autochthonous and wives regarded as "foreigners." American Harry Gailey, an African historian, comment on the influence of women's "foreign" status in the society; "In addition to their influential roles as wives and mothers, they were accustomed to being consulted on issues affecting the village . . . Their work as traders took them beyond the narrow confines of their own villages and this combined with exogamy gave the women of one village the ability to influence other women over a wide range."[67]

---

66. Spohn, *What are they Saying*, 87.
67. Gailey, *The Road to Aba*, 100.

Women's influence outside the confines of their marital homes, particularly their control of trade and commerce would become critical to their socio-political struggle in the nascent years of colonization. It became a vital communication channel. Because women could send messages across the land through the market network, they were able to gather women from all of Eastern Nigeria in a short notice. They came together as a group in 1929 to protest against the British colonial administration in the region. The protest is what has since been termed *Ogu Umunwanyi*; Women's War. *Ogu Umunwanyi* represents a marker in African women's modern history. Suppressed for decades in historical annals and never taught in Nigerian schools, this defining socio-political event began gaining attention in recent years.[68] At some level, *Ogu Umunwanyi* responded to the question *Ejinwanyiemenini* "what can one do with a female." The event demonstrated and publicly stated not only to the Igbo society but also to the larger patriarchal culture *what the female can do*.

Ogu Umunwanyi, Women's War, 1929—1931

Ogu Umunwanyi erupted as a response to colonial repression. Several factors led to the episode. According to the Nigeria historian, S. N. Nwabara, these include the proposed imposition of direct tax on women. A discontent caused by the taxation of men as well as the dissatisfaction at the persecution, extortion, and corruption practiced by Native Court members.[69] The emerging economy was another major factor that fuelled the discontent. Chief among these was the colonial policy of lower prices for domestic products and higher prices of imported goods.[70] But the underlying factor remained a blatant compromising of women's traditional role in leadership and the control of the market system by the new administration. Thus, after several attempts at peaceful negotiations with the colonial administration failed, women in Eastern Nigeria represented themselves by an act of war against the colonial administration.

Ogu Umunwanyi disclosed as well as demonstrated to the British colonial administration a picture of women in Igbo and Ibibio societies that they never could have imagined. Lord Frederick Lugard, the then

---

68. Nzegwu, "Recovering Igbo Tradition," 451.
69. Nwabara, *Iboland*, 181.
70. Nwabara, *Iboland*, 181.

British Governor-General of Nigeria, described the event as a "strange phenomenon."[71] Lugard, like most Western colonizers, had an image of women that represented absolute submission, which the Christian "household code" tends to fosters (cf. Col 3:18–4:1; Eph 5:21–6:9; Titus 2:1–10; 1 Peter 2:18–3:7). A certain interpretation of the Code makes women into the handmaiden of the male. In the mind of Lugard, therefore, women should stay at home, submit to the will of the colonial officials and their husbands, and essentially renounce their political and economic rights. This was impossible for the traditional women who had been used to managing their own affairs without meddling from men, African or European.[72] The women knew the effect of male monopoly and the power of the economy. They knew that if they became economically vulnerable and beholden to men their social worth and dignity would be undercut severely. So they opposed any decision that promoted divesting them of full participation in the social economy.

The women demonstrated visibility and vocality. They spoke to the highest authority in the land, the colonialist, and in so doing, showed that neither traditional patriarchy nor ingrained subordination found in names such as *Ejinwanyiemenini*, *Nwanyikwa* or *Nwanyibuife*, could silence them. Their courage is likened to that of the biblical *doulas*, women of faith and courage such as Judith. Judith risked her life to save the dignity of her people, to rescue her town Bethulia, from the destructive forces of Nebuchadnezzar at a time when the men of the city were ready to give up the fight. In like manner, women in Igboland asserted their traditional role as savior figures and defended Igbo dignity against inimical foreign socio-political incursion. This singular accomplishment on the part of the women responded in part to the question *Ejinwanyiemenini*? What can one do with a female child?

In tens of thousands, all across Eastern Nigeria, women demonstrated their ability by marching to the District Headquarter in Aba. As in most war situations, women suffered causalities. Nevertheless, they succeeded in redefining the "synthetic political structure maintained by the British."[73] The commission's report, published in July 1930 went so far as to compare this movement to that of the British suffragettes. The

---

71. Nzegwu, *Family Matters*, 79.
72. Davidson, *Africa in History*, 181.
73. Gailey, *The Road to Aba*, 97.

message was heard, and starting on this date the colonial authorities introduced a few women into the native courts.[74]

British educationist and the wife of a colonial official Sylvia Leith-Ross, describes "what women can do" in a reflection on *Ogu Umunwanyi*. Leith-Ross, who lived through the experience, describes *Ogu Umunwanyi* participants as a "rare and invaluable force . . . ambitious, go-ahead, courageous, self-reliant, hardworking, independent women."[75] She recognizes the women's startling energy and their power of organization and of leadership, their practical common sense and quick apprehension of reality. She contends that the women protesters were bound to take a leading role in the development of Nigeria. Regrettably, Leith-Ross's prediction has not quite happened. Another Briton, Margaret Green, reminiscences about *Ogu Umunwanyi*: "One hears Europeans talking of 'these matriarchies of West Africa' where, in popular imagination, fierce Amazons or wise and powerful grandmothers hold sway over tribes of apparently unprotesting males. The Aba women's riots of 1929—31 did nothing to counteract this view."[76] These wise and powerful women expressed agency even in a society where naming is employed to keep them down. Regardless of metaphors that disparaging names foster, the women's response to what they perceived as an invading culture, remains an eloquent testimony in countering the name designation, *Ejinwanwanyiemenini*?

The surfacing of pejorative names such as *Ejinwanyiemenini*, "what can one do with a female," raises a fundamental question concerning the composition of African communities. Do Africans still believe that women have no value, or that they are not counted? Should women remain where they are, presumably locked up by culture and custom? These intimations produce a crisis of identity in women. Such was the conflict the character of Beatrice *Nwanyibuife* confronted in her earlier years; she perceived her given name, *Nwanyibuife*, to be fudged. Because a person's identity represents her most treasured possession, the struggle to claim and maintain identity corresponds to the human craving for meaning. This search for identity sustains the female-child in the fight for self-identification. African women's reflection on Mary, who identifies herself as the *doulē kyriou* and follows through with her new personality

74. Coquery-Vidrovitch, *African Women*, 164.
75. Leith-Ross, *Southern African Women*, 19–20.
76. Green, *Ibo Village Affairs*, 139.

in the singular act of prophecy in the hill country, provides a model of positive self-identification. The *doulē* metaphor, therefore, demonstrates that women have creative powers, which gives them a core of identity, self-motivation, or autonomy and redemption.

Renaming the Girl-Child

The Benin theologian Valentin Dedji states that African social engineering has evolved a system in which individuals define themselves in terms of their relationship with others.[77] Assuming such to be the case, what is the role of names which create a psychological distance?

In *Anthills*, Achebe provides the metaphoric lens through which to engage renaming the female-child. He proposes the name *Amaechina*, may-the-path-never-close. Symbolically, a female girl functions always and in all respects as the "traffic" that keeps the path open. *Amaechina* reflects an Akan (Ghana) proverb, "Without women 'a lineage is finished'."[78] In effect, *Amaechina* announces a continuous flow, a renewal.

The circumstances surrounding the naming of *Amaechina* remain significant to the female narrative. In the novel, the author assigns the privilege of naming to the great uncle of the newborn. But the new energies emerging from the "alternative community" redescribe the event. At the suggestion of Beatrice *Nwanyibuife*, the remnant names the infant before the arrival of the designated name giver.

The birth and name of the newborn represent another strange phenomenon. Achebe remains unconventional in breaking with the literary ethos that generally creates a male-child at the end of a tragic tale. Generally, the male continues the family line, hence the name, *Amaechina*. The author's exceptional creativity represents that opening through which women in contemporary Igbo society seek to make connection with the rich Igbo past. The association with this "strange phenomenon" represents the outcry that women ought to demonstrate in the formation of an alternative community, where women's narrative reflects positive images of what women can do. The designated name giver, the great uncle of the newborn, understands the dawn of a new beginning in Kanga, seizes the moment and states pithily, "Do you know why I am laughing like this? I am laughing because in you young people

---

77. Dedji, *Reconstruction and Renewal*, 67.
78. Oduyoye, *Daughters of Anowa*, 7.

our world has met its match. Yes! You have put the world where it should sit... My wife here was breaking her head looking for kolanuts, for alligator pepper, for honey and for bitter-leaf... And while she is cracking her head you people gather in this whiteman house and give a girl a boy's name . . . This is how to handle the world."[79] The elder convincingly proclaims the inauguration of the future. He challenges contemporary female name-givers to take cognizance of the *signs of the times* and claim the possibility that "the other world" offers. Markedly, naming a girl-child *Amaechina*, a traditionally male name, hits at the root metaphor of social reconstruction. Furthermore, the name, *Amaechina*, for a girl-child fulfills the male-daughter tradition, retrieved and rewoven for a modern context.

Structurally, the name *Amaechina* constitutes a shift. The shift in this case represents a change from one way of thinking about women to another; something of a revolution, a transformation. The change in *Anthills* was driven by agents of change, specifically the failed patriarchal hegemonic hold on society. The name and naming ceremony registers this shift, which can have potent social consequences for the Igbo society. In a typical metaphoric logic, the name *Amaechina* responds to and subverts the name *Nwanyibuife*.

Naming the female-child in contemporary idiom admits another possibility. Modern female names that do not reflect women's self-understanding in current idiom risk implicating women in their own subjugation. Like the Hebrew, Igbo language connotes rather than denotes. Both languages have stronger connotation than denotation potential than is accredited to the English and the Western use of language. Similarly, the Igbo language points and opens and suggests, but does not conclude or define, therefore, attention to the subtlety of Igbo language remains critical in fashioning female names.[80] The power of naming that Mary receives (Luke1:31) and exercises reinforces her position as *doulē*. In the Annunciation narrative, the author introduces her as Mary, the maiden from the township of Nazareth (Luke 1:27). In the verse that follows, Gabriel names her "the favored one." Towards the end of narrative, Mary, the favored one, names herself *doulē kyriou*, the servant of the LORD (Luke 1:38). The new name emerges from a multiple narrative, not only from her village background as a young betrothed, but also her

---

79. Achebe, *Anthills*, 227.
80. Brueggemann, *Word Militant*, 149.

spiritual awakening occasioned by the angelic encounter. Mary's integrated narrative informs her growing self-understanding as servant of God, prophet and leader of God's new people. Thus reconstructing the identity of women in Igbo society always will involve multiple narratives grounded in contemporary history with a sense of the future.

Retelling: The Story

When I first thought of writing this story, I shared the prospects with a colleague. The response I received was, why now, you mean after 30 years of religious life, you still question what the Handmaid represents Handmaid. I responded to him with a story, a tortoise story.

A tortoise fell into a pit. It was not an empty pit. The pit was a cesspool. After remaining in the pit for seven years (seven is the symbolic holy number), someone discovered that the tortoise has been missing and had been in this horrifying condition for a long time. As the rescue process was underway to get the tortoise from the cesspool, there was a slight delay. For the tortoise, however, the slight delay seemed like a thousand years. The yearning to be free again, to reclaim its imperiled dignity, impelled the poor tortoise to yell at the top of its lungs, from the depths, "Please get me out of here. I can no longer tolerate the stench in this pit!" Mind you, this was its seventh year of a humiliating existence, and, I must add, seven long years of uncommon fortitude.

Tortoise stories form perhaps the largest corpus of African-Igbo moral narratives. One can find a close parallel between the tortoise tale and the women's less than positive experience in general. That women are constructed, marginalized, deprived of certain rights, and ignored in certain circles remains a fact that stares humanity in the face and confronts gender relations. Like the proverbial tortoise, the situations in which women have lived for decades do not appear to penetrate their shell. In some way, hope of a newness has kept women's inner-self intact. The tortoise attitude on the day of "liberation" suggests that the vexing conditions remained on the outside.

Most women like the tortoise, do not consider themselves to be permanently stained by the experience of exclusion and marginalization. But they do want a way out. Such a way involves securing their dignity which has been threatened by being absentees in ongoing history. This sense of dignity protects women from internalizing their untoward environment. Women know that no person or situation can take away dignity. Dignity is ingrained in self-hood. Just as in the tortoise tale, when the time came to assert the rights that protects its dignity it could no longer be silent, it yelled, "Please get me out of this pit." The sense of dignity impelled the tortoise to cry out. Women's uncommon fortitude had enabled them not to be indoctrinated by the situation in which the dominant voice in society, for the most part, has placed them. By maintaining its dignity in an extremely difficult situation, the tortoise affirmed that the sense of self resides within. The attempt to reach within informed the retrieval and reconstruction processes and interrogating root metaphors, particularly name texts, which forms the collective social consciousness of most African peoples.

Retelling stories, Nkoli, suggests that the primary mode by which the African communities reconstitute themselves represent telling and reinterpreting or deconstructing its narratives. The stories women live, which they narrate, become the higher narratives, as Ben Okri puts it that assist the soul to fly up toward the greater light.[81] These accounts appear in form of diachronic and synchronic that is to say the difference between the past and the present, and the similarities. Reading Scripture from these perspectives enriches a community's reflection on ancient memories and tradition. The reflecting community recasts its memory and tradition in new ways that remain resonant with the new situation, a form of reweaving that makes contemporaneous the older tradition. Schüsler Fiorenza echoes similar thought in encouraging women's voice: "In every generation women have to challenge anew the patriarchal definition of reality, we have to speak "to reinvent the wheel" over and over again because patriarchy cannot tolerate the conscientization of the oppressed."[82] Reinventing the wheel suggests continuous reweaving, a constant retelling of women's positive actions in the community. The spinning wheel, where the threads for the stories emerge, is the very embodiment of women's life in their continual self-gift for the common good. Such retelling validates present actions of subjects and announces hope for the future.

Retelling represents the greatest act of rememorializing. The bulk of biblical literature constitutes such retelling (cf. Deut 6:7).[83] The Bible, a story of liberation, tells of a community's struggle for peoplehood. The

---

81. Okri, *Way of Being Free*, 126.
82. Schüsler Fiorenza, "Breaking the Silence," 172.
83. Frizzell, "Mary's Magnificat: Source and Themes," 38–59.

Magnificat of the *doulē kyriou* "reinvents" or retells Israel's prophetic tradition (Luke 1:42–55). New Testament writings represent the narratives of a people seeking to reconstitute the community in the face of new dangers. In a similar manner, women in Igbo society must dream dreams and produce narratives that reflect their struggle of self-becoming for the present age. Such narratives of necessity will involve interrogating root metaphors, those primary tools employed to construct language and the concepts of existence. Moreover, humans cannot escape language because we experience, interpret and understand reality through it. Therefore, since language shapes reality, society must choose carefully language that recognizes as well as honors value. Such an approach can deal decisively with the choosing and giving of female names.

Since the idea of name as a marker still has a hermeneutical purchase in Igbo society, debasing female names that have passed into cultural idioms demands retrieving, deconstructing and ultimately reconstructing. Engaging and dismantling disenabling structures from their deepest foundation, therefore, requires critical retelling and interpretation.

THE DOULĒ METAPHOR REVISITED

The word "Handmaid," read as the one who accompanies in a subordinate position, under represents its potential significance. In its contemporary usage, the word signifies domestication. Such understanding fosters women's silence and invisibility. Like the proverbial tortoise rescued from the cesspool, years of domestication engendered by the interpretation of the word, Handmaid may soon be a thing of the past. This can happen only if women can claim their call as *doulē kyriou*, Servants of the LORD. Such representation and interpretation of the handmaid makes imperative this redemptive narrative.

A redemptive narrative goes deep into the stories that have formed our Christian religious consciousness. It begins with the Book of Genesis. In rethinking women's role in contemporary society, Achebe compares a patriarchal assigned role to women in the Hebrew Scripture and in the New Testament. He likens women's reduced status to the Christian perception of Eve in the Book of Genesis. Achebe contends that in the New Testament, the process of women's degradation later translated motherhood into an object of exaltation.

Therefore, the idea came to man to turn his spouse into the very Mother of God, to pick her up from right under his foot where she'd been since Creation and carry her reverently to a nice, corner pedestal. Up there, her feet completely off the ground she will be just as irrelevant to the practical decisions of running the world as she was in the bad old days. The only difference is that now man will suffer no guilt feelings; he can sit back and congratulate himself on his generosity and gentlemanliness.[84]

There is no denying that certain interpretations employ the image of Mary in the New Testament to foster women's subordination. Mary's celebrated submission to God in Luke 1:38 represent a case in point. I, however, challenge such literalistic and uncritical perception of Mary. The symbolism of Mary so intricately woven into the tapestry of Roman Catholic religious imagination evokes a variety of rich significance.

A critical evaluation of the *Magnificat*, for example, reveals that Mary should not be "on a pedestal," removed from the life of women in the Roman Catholic Church, and society of every age. English Anglican clergyman Paul Avis supports this Roman Catholic idea of Mary. He, however, opines that the image of Mary remains more relevant in Catholicism than in Protestantism. For him, in Catholicism, Mary and the Church belong to the heavenly realm and the sacramental ministry, with its washing and feeding, counterbalancing the dominating male symbols of God.[85] Avis' notion of Mary supports the arguments of her role as *doulē kyriou*, a servant as well as leader, that continues to function as model of self-identification for men and women as servants in the community. Avis further argues that in Protestantism, Mary and the Church remain reduced to the human level—weak, mortal, fallible— and the ministry is conceived in terms of the male activity of preaching the word.[86] This suggestion of Mary as separate from reality coheres with the insights of Presbyterian biblical scholar Judy Siker. Siker asserts that with the exception of a brief appearance every December, Mary has remained virtually absent from Protestant life and faith.[87] It is evident, therefore, that the symbolism of Mary of Nazareth in her assertion as the *doulē kyriou* institutes a new paradigm for all Christians.

84. Achebe, *Anthills*, 98.
85. Avis, *Eros and the Sacred*, 20.
86. Avis, *Eros and the Sacred*.
87. Siker, "Blessed One: Protestant Perspective on Mary," 559.

Conclusion

Naming constitutes a very powerful rhetorical tool in the construction of personal and social identities. Names as root metaphor have a kind of perennial power to evoke a response. Certain names generate new metaphors that cluster around and enrich them and draw vitality from them. The naming of the female-child served well in this regard. Such naming provided the semantic structures that have continued to sustain patriarchal sexism. Drawing from the oracle of Jeremiah 1:10, the women in Igbo society can begin to rebuild the Igbo semantic field in an attempt to reinterpret languages that tend to oppress and dehumanize women, thereby, impoverishing society as a whole. Certain aspects of the Igbo material culture, particularly in the precolonial period, provide opportunities to explore symbols that can be redemptive. Although precolonial times span millennia, very little information exists about the period. Materials preserved in writings, paintings, names, rituals, and oral literature represents an insignificant amount of information of the expanse of time. Narratives celebrating social and religious activities of women during the early years of colonization provide a window into the Igbo past and women's role during that epoch. Such stories furnish the lens with which to engage the names that degrade women. Specifically, recalling narratives of women's positive contribution to society represents a form of resistance to repressive policies as well as a call to the future. Metaphor and myth employed to silence and marginalize women begin to fall apart in the retelling of these narratives.

A realistic vision of women in Igbo society remains connected with their passion, compassion, imagination, and inspiration. These qualities compel women to reject, oppose, and resist limitations that the dominant culture tends to impose on their imaginations. If to poison a nation means poisoning its narratives, it does imply that non-liberating stories, whether in elaborate tales or name texts, have devastating consequences. If to poison a nation means poisoning its narratives, it does imply that non-liberating stories, whether in elaborate tales or in name text, have devastating consequences. Uncontaminated narratives, however, have the potential to transport to another world of infinite possibilities, the uwa-tu-uwa, where the imagination comes to life. Uncontaminated narratives, however, have the potential to transport to another world of infinite possibilities, the *uwa-tu-uwa*, where the imagination comes to life. Therefore, redemptive readings of texts that can be oppressive provide women in contemporary Igbo society the tool to construct positive models of self-identification. Therefore, redemptive readings of texts that can be oppressive provide women in contemporary Igbo society the tool to construct positive models of self-identification. In the final and concluding chapter, I recapitulate such reading. I employ examples of *doulas* characters that provide images that can facilitate appropriation for transformation. I contend that only such transformation can quicken women's fuller engagement in social processes.

5

The *Doulē*: Biblical and Contemporary

Introduction

REMAKING HISTORY TO SUIT current identity begins with questioning that which is considered the dominant version of reality. The dominant version dictates the way things "ought" to be. The inquiring position I have taken in this book, represents one such questioning exercise that can lead to transformation. But transformation comes with appropriation. Remaking history fits into the notion of appropriation. Appropriation cannot be confused with adaptation. Adaptation, describes an evolutionary process whereby a population becomes better suited to an environment. Thus adaptation produces more or less a hybrid. But appropriation implies the practice of making one's own that which genuinely belongs to another. Cultural tourists, for example, do so all the time. They go to another culture, and partake of their ceremonies, foods, and customs and then appropriate it to enhance their way of life. In this way, their culture becomes richer, finer and more beautiful. Appropriation in the context of the biblical women I discussed in this book, however, demands a critical drawing back from the biblical text to approximate a meeting of the world of the reader and that of the text. The world of the text, represented in the metaphor of the *doulē* in Luke 1:26–38, yields a variety of scenarios. Each synopsis can lend itself to a diverse degree of appropriation in reimaging women in a contemporary society and Church life. To reconstitute women's role, particularly in Africa, the traditional and contemporary religious traditions must be put together in dialogue. The discussion in this final and concluding chapter is in the form of a mosaic that continues the women's discourse.

The interest in this chapter, therefore, involves weaving a fabric that is representative of women's fuller humanity. *Akwete*, a rich cloth indigenous to Igboland, could represent the contemporary *doulē*. These intense, differentiated, beautiful, and sturdy cloths function metaphorically in representing idioms that foster fullness of life and the common good. But most especially, the *akwete* cloth symbolizes images of positive self-identification for women. The intense and sturdy representation of women in the Lukan Gospel narrative, asserts God's liberative work in history. The hermeneutical approaches applied in the Lukan passage, yield insights that make possible a reintroduction of women as representatives and agents of God's saving action in the community of humankind. The protagonist of this story, Mary of Nazareth, the *doulē kyriou*, represents that prototype to which many Christian women aspire. The hope, therefore, is that the discussion on these pages brings to the ordinary person, women and men, of faith an appreciation of Mary of Nazareth, the prototype of service, in everyday life and not only as an object of devotion.

Spohn states that "prototypes undergo development when they are applied to new situations, and these new applications bring out aspects that were latent in the original or even at variance with its presuppositions."[1] This idea of prototype holds for both moral and religious archetypes. Spohn's insight provides the lens through which to negotiate appropriating the metaphor of the *doulē* proposed in this book. In retrieving and weaving together values that speak of women's positive role from both biblical and Igbo cultural patterns, one can facilitate a reconstruction of the image of the Handmaid distorted by uncritical interpretations of texts, texts texts meaning written words, symbols, visual arts, social systems, and the myths which maintain them. The modest setting of the Lukan narrative permits readers to take "the view from below."[2] Only from such a privileged position of viewing from below, can social changes occur because it prioritizes the social location of those on the margin, represented by the poor and the oppressed. In so doing, the privileged position of those on the margins becomes the advantaged source of theology and social reconstruction. Commitment to social change, therefore, leads to transformation and a challenging knowledge of God.

A transformative and challenging knowledge of God is that which women seek. In the African societies that have become increasingly

1. Spohn, *Go and Do Likewise*, 119.
2. Spohn, *Go and Do Likewise*.

Christianized, Scripture becomes the starting point in reconceptualizing societal identity. Scripture's currency in Africa provides the vantage point from which to rearticulate a new vision of women. Because the primary aim of biblical interpretation focuses on the glory of God and the edification of the reader, a Scripture rendering that enhances life, celebrates that glory. Such representation of Scripture agrees with the theology of Church Father, Irenaeus, who contends that the glory of God is a human being fully alive.[3] Listening to certain interpretation of some Scriptural texts reveals many thoughts left unstated. It implies that there is much "unfinished business" in biblical interpretation. The new business means that we must glean what the major harvesters have inadvertently left behind. The gleaning process brings to the fore that which remains implicit in the text. The gleaned elements provide the strands that make up the woof which we can creatively employ to reimage women's role in contemporary African society. The indigenous traditions, on the other hand, form the warp. Thus biblical and indigenous traditions form the warp and woof of the metaphoric *akwete* cloth. The warp is variegated from being dyed in many different local patterns. The color of the warp changes in combination with the woof as it is seen. While there is no alteration in the actual color of the fibers, the eye interprets them differently when they realigned with another color-this is the beauty of the *Akwete*. Like taffeta, which shines differently from different angles, and derives a third color from the combination of warp and woof, *Akwete* has a similar shifting pattern dependent on how the cloth is draped and how it is viewed.

I have organized this concluding discussion in four sections. The focus of the first two sections is on women as subjects of ongoing history as well as the ideal prophetic community in which women could flourish. I discuss further Mary of Nazareth and the woman of Shunem as images demanding appropriation for the contemporary *doulas*. The example of Mother Mary Charles Walker, Religious Sister of Charity (RSC) and the Religious community she founded in 1931, the Congregation of the Handmaid of the Holy Child Jesus in the third section, represents a modern example of *doulas* figures. The fourth section focuses on the woman in the global village. I continue with a concrete example of the women in Igbo society. Each aspect of this chapter represents an aspect of the mosaic or a strand that can enhance the fabric that is representa-

---

3. Irenaeus, *Adversus Haereses*, Book 4, 6.

tive of women's fuller humanity and participants as subjects in ongoing history.

REVISITING BIBLICAL REFLECTIONS: THE *DOULĒ* OF NAZARETH

The Bible constitutes much of the religious context in contemporary African societies. The presence of the Bible in Africa lends credence to employing biblical imaginations in contributing to the reconstruction of the image of women in African society and Church life. A reading of Mary of Nazareth in the Lukan passage offers new perspectives in proposing that critical evaluation of texts could sustain constructing a positive contemporary image of women, particularly among African Christians. The normative principle for reading Scripture, however, cannot be derived from the text alone. As a living tradition, such authority must come from the experience of the community as well. Thus women's experience remains critical to the arguments presented in this book.

Scripture is for the enrichment of the community. The connection between the moral meaning of the scriptural text in its setting and its current meaning must be in the community. Scripture is not static. It implies a contemporary faith experience that activates and enlivens relationships at all levels of human endeavor. As a believing community, therefore, a contextual reading of the sacred text provides the grounding in the faith that humans seek to possess in their life and undertakings. Thus the privileged place of tradition becomes indispensable in the hermeneutical process. Only from this stance can women's appropriation of the *doulē* metaphor make sense because such appropriation of the sacred text comes from their experience of contemporary struggle. Valuing women's experience in the understanding of the sacred text constitutes women as subjects rather than objects of interpretation. New perspectives of thought and action within the tradition of the *doulē* emerge with women as the subject and prerogative of the interpretation. Thus, reflecting on Scripture from women's experience liberates them from the burden imposed by the dominant androcentric version of biblical interpretation, as well as men's theological reflection as the only source of spiritual enlightenment.

Another form of contextual reading also can become non-liberating depending on the interpretive agenda of the hermeneutist. An agendum that furthers the ideology of subordination represents a source of intimidation. In the service of religion, individuals can be intimated to abdicate responsibility for their own lives. Such a thought is inconsistent with the *doulas* figures that Luke consciously represents both in his Gospel and in the Acts of the Apostles. The Nazareth *doulē*, whose agency culminated in self-gift, confirms that only a subject who possesses dignity is capable of such action. Agency employed here represents the ability to act. To have agency means having a moral imperative because one has will. Thus religious practices, rather than an instrument that softens for the kill, provide avenues for greater self awareness as the lives of the biblical *doulas* strongly suggests. But that there must be understanding requires qualification.

While faith tradition, expressed in religious practices, enables the active engagement with the text, a certain amount of suspicion must prevail to engage critically the text if we desire to elicit meaning for the transformation of lives. Thus, a critical reading of Scripture allows the honing of religious beliefs. Such rendering sharpens the understanding of the expression "Word of God." The Word of God functions as metaphor.[4] A perception of the metaphor provides the means by which different people can embrace its meaning, as well as appropriate its insights. Many "Bible people," women in particular, however, remain still caught in the first naiveté; that is to say, they understand the Bible to be literally the Word of God. Such inadequate appreciation of the biblical text has continued to inform the receptivity of the content of the message. A low receptivity of the content of the biblical message invariably means a loss of significance to the audience of the profound meaning of the Good News.

A literal reading of Scripture leads many, women as well as men, to appropriate Mary's consent in Luke 1:38, "Be it done unto me according to your word," as complete submission. The idea of absolute submission can depict the position of the disciple. What is at stake, however, is the self-understanding of the subject that produces such a total response. The question then is whether Mary was active or passive in her act of disciple-becoming?

Undoubtedly, passivity does not characterize Mary in the passage under review, Luke 1:26–38. Mary's active participation in the process is evidenced in her conversation with the angel Gabriel. She categorically was not compliant. Her obedience was a compliance that was open to the

---

4. Schneiders, *Revelatory Text*, 169.

future, an agreement that was filled with potential. This particular action establishes Mary's obedience as an act of supreme activity. Undermining the dialogical relationship through which the "Word was made Flesh," raises a problem. It undercuts the human faith aspect of the story and has a potential that undermines human flourishing.

The narrative shows that Mary flourished progressively. Her prophetic role took form amidst uncertain circumstances. Her perception of the situation awakened in her awareness that deep pondering sustained. Note that the evocation that meditative silence denoted in this episode represented a liminal stage in approaching discipleship. In silence the faith that sought understanding began to take form. After pondering in her heart, Mary spoke (Luke 1:34). Thus a deliberate thought process precedes a meaningful action. It does mean that Mary's attempt in seeking understanding came from a deep personal reflection engendered by a profound silence. She showed by her action that the disciple engages the world only after a profound pondering in the heart.

A further analysis of the *doulē* metaphor in her complete submission reveals deeper truths. Mary's obedience was not in response to a collection of timeless divine rules. Rather the episode provided the shape to which the life of the Christian should correspond, that of *being*— "how can this be?" (Luke 1:34). The awareness of *being* resides in the groundbreaking question, how can it be? The inquiry implicitly denotes listening. Listening closely relates to obedience (*abaudire* in Latin where *audire* means to listen). Thus the availability to be receptive to the Word points to a preparedness to do it, meaning to obey (parere). Listening, therefore, suggests half-way obedience towards what one really hears.

Mary hears the angel's message. She obeys as would a steward. The steward in this sense describes the one who at once takes as well as gives orders (Luke 12:42). A critical reading of the Annunciation story divulges the taking and the giving of orders. It reveals that the divine command requests permission before it becomes a command. It was a dialogue, an inter-relational activity. According to Spohn, such permission "corresponds to the central quality that God has manifested in history, namely, graciousness." Spohn goes on to state that "Divine commands will be experienced primarily as positive gifts rather than obligations. A gracious permission enables our response by granting us the freedom to *be* in a specific direction."[5] In effect, fundamental obedience supports the

5. Spohn, *Go and Do Likewise*, 33.

freedom *to be* and to do. This sense of the freedom *to be* and to do questions the idea of uncritical obedience. Insistence on swift obedience in certain circles grossly undermine the dialogical relationship represented in this foundational Christian narrative, the Incarnation.

Further reflections on the Lukan passage yield a certain newness deriving from this foundational narrative. If appropriation follows the "arrow of meaning" in a text to engender a new understanding, God's declaration of newness stands out in the bare dissimilarity between the characters of Zachariah and Mary. The author contrasts the two in terms of gender, age, social and religious status. He prepares the reader for the reversal that God is about to accomplish through the teenage Jewish maiden. Luke builds the distinction by contrasting Zachariah, an older male figure, a priest who serves in the sanctuary with the triteness of Mary's village background. While the older male married temple priest represented the dominant version of full personhood, one who could participant fully in social processes, the young female yet-to-be-married villager became a participant in a greater process, a progenitor of the new People of God. This way, Mary outshone the "institutional" Zachariah on all fronts; a sign of that newness God declares (Luke 4:18–19; John 20:17–18). Clearly, Good news is not suggestive of patriarchal overlordship.

Under patriarchy there exists an implicit belief that men represent the sacred and women participate in the sacred things. Luke exposes such assumption. But such thought continues to linger on. Indeed, English Protestant Clergyman, Paul Avis, reaffirms the tradition that women participate in the sacred only through the mediation of their husbands, fathers, or male priests?[6] In the Lukan narrative (1:26–38), Mary demonstrated that women could become representatives of the sacred without participation in the sanctuary. Although Mary's role as *Theotokos*, Mother of God, positioned her as a symbol of the sacred, her sacredness emerged not only from being a mother but from the service which she rendered. Motherhood represents service to another because, "From their experience of service as mothers, women move to the experience of community, burst the confining limits of their domestic tasks and discover themselves as creators of history.[7] The concept of motherhood is not synonymous with that of the *doulē*; rather it is but a role

---

6. Avis, *Eros and the Sacred*, 151.

7. Tepedino and Brandao, "Women and the Theology of Liberation," 224.

of the *doulē*. Mary represented a channel of grace not because of her biological role as mother, but by her social role, that of servant of God (Luke 1:38).

By serving, Mary mediated the sacred. Being a symbol of the sacred, Mary became a channel of grace. She becomes a model of self-identification for women who may not need to identify with the sanctuary to attain personhood. In Mary's circumstance, we witness the newness and beauty which could emanate "from below." Mary's story in the Lukan passage brings to light a newness whose source emerges from those outside the dominant group, women. The prophetic declaration of the *Magnificat* (Luke 1:46–55), in a capsule form, proclaimed those "below" as subjects of ongoing history. Another piece of the mosaic is a story of a woman in the second book of Kings. In the interaction with the prophet Elisha, we observe another Israel's *doulē*, the woman of Shunem, who represents a retrievable element that can be appropriated.

THE WOMAN OF SHUNEM (2 KGS 4:8–37)

The cultural context of ancient Israel provides the language of appropriating the *doulē* metaphor as we showed in chapter two. This narrative of the prophet Elisha and the Shunammite, brings to the fore another example of a small town *doulē* figure. The story shows a classic example of the intricacies in the everyday life of an Israelite woman, a narrative that resonates with many women in the Two-Thirds world. In this short narrative, the author of 2 Kings shows the scope and fluidity of relationship within this ancient community, considered strictly patriarchal.

The narrator employs cultural norms, customs, and patterns of relationships that form the structures that define women's placement in society. Cultures that place a premium on relationship can identify with this little tale. Fundamentally, relationships entail concern for community as well as hospitality. The culture takes seriously and sensitively relatedness and inter-relatedness that touch on reciprocity, mutuality, and justice that community living demands.[8] Such a culture provides for the appropriate environment an enabling factor that engenders the flourishing of women as well as men.

The unnamed woman of Shunem exemplified one such person who flourished in this culture. Scripture points to her being a person of influ-

---

8. Oduyoye, *Introducing*, 32.

ence and of wealth. This small town woman received and showed the prophet Elisha, a man of God, hospitality. Wanting to do more for the prophet, the woman consulted with her husband. They both provided the man of God a comfortable rooftop room in their home as a rest stop. The prophet can have an overnight stay whenever he passed by. Not wanting to be outdone in generosity, the prophet reciprocated. As the story goes, the prophet, comprehending the woman's ability, offered her a possibility of wider exposure. He wants to introduce her to the top brass, the King and the military commander: "You have lavished all this care on us; what can we do for you? Can we say a good word for you to the king or to the commander of the army?" (v. 14). Evidently, the man of God noted that his host, the woman of Shunem, possessed startling qualities and a power of organization and of leadership that could support development beyond her small town. She could be of greater influence in a wider context. Thus he proposed to say a good word about her to the authorities. In effect, Elisha was recommending her for a higher official position, a position that would likely take her out of her small town.

The prophet noted that the woman's quick sense of comprehension and veracity would fit not only into the higher civil society, but also in the military, a thought that is reminiscence of the prophet and Judge, Deborah in the book of Judges (Jdgs 4 – 5). Deborah is the only female prophet mentioned in the Book of the Former Prophets. In the book of Judges, she emerged the hero of the conflict with Sisera's army. The Song of Deborah in chapter 5 of the book of Judges is a hymn celebrating victory over Sisera's army. This song is considered one of the oldest texts of the Bible. Judge Deborah stood among Israel's morally upright prophetic leaders in the tradition of Moses, Joshua, Gideon, and Samuel. Judges and prophets were charismatic leaders and including Deborah in this ancient text shows that these roles were open to women of her time. It took a prophetic mind to note that the Shunammite woman was truly versatile. Given the state of national security at the period, the prophet sensed the woman's acute sense of leadership, thinking she could support Israel's military. This revolutionary idea can only come from a prophet. He even suggests that the king also needs her talents. Elisha's proposal allows one to evaluate the relationship between the prophet and the leadership, civil and military, in the Israel of his day.

But the Shunammite turned down the prophet's offer. "I am living among my own people," she replied (v. 13). She rejected the establishment. Like a typical *doulē*, the woman opted to remain in solidarity with those "below," those outside the dominant institution, her small town folks. She would neither go to the king nor the commander of the army. She remained attached with the small town people, whose solidarity may have perhaps shaped her. The Shunammite *doulē* represented herself as a servant. "Living among my own people" could mean that service to the nation is not location bound. For her, service in a small environment, is of value with service rendered on a national level, in this case, to the commander of the army or of the king.

The narrative points to the significance of service in the community. Service emerges from the ethos of hospitality, solidarity, reciprocity, and mutuality. While the woman and her husband served Elisha by providing hospitality, Elisha also served the family. Later in the narrative the prophet makes another offer to the family, this time offering the woman a promise of a progeny, "This time next year you will be fondling a baby son" (v.16). Note that the prophet deals exclusively with the woman even in the most delicate matter of bringing forth a progeny. Again, Elisha's actions support the radical nature of prophetic utterances. Progeny, however, does not seem to be of a desperate concern to the woman, "'Please, my lord,' she protested, 'you are a man of God; do not deceive your servant'" (v. 16). Her earlier reaction to the prophet "I am living among my own people," suggests that the Shunammite woman seemed content with serving in her local community. When the "gift-son" died, the woman made haste to the home of Elisha. On finding him, she chided the prophet demanding, "Did I ask my lord for a son?" (v. 28). Her reaction when the gift-child died supports my assertion.

It does appear that the Shunammite did not perceive the offer of a progeny as an enhancement of social status. She already had influence in her community. The *doulē* also had rights within the body politic, hence her assertion of staying with her own people. The Shunammite's claim to influence does not involve power in its politicized meaning. Politicized power can represent a means of oppression and a tool employed to trample on the humanity of another. The authoritarian concept of power is antithetical to the concept of the *doulē*. For the most part, women do not seek to acquire instruments that discriminate and dominate. Perhaps the idea of power in the sense of dominating that came from the king's circle or the military garrison informed the woman of Shunem to reject the prophet's offer. What women seek and indeed, must seek, points to a down-to-earth approach to service. As people of faith, service represents the only instrument that has the ability to unite people and guarantee human flourishing. Service represents the instrument of solidarity and symbolizes that which defines the people of faith, "Behold, I am the handmaid of the Lord, May it be done to me according to your word" (Luke 1:38). In addition, the only way Jesus' presence is felt in the community of believers constitutes service, "I am among you as one who serves" (Luke 22:27). Service, the quintessential quality of the *doulē*, represents an intense engagement with life, agency, and a quality that the woman of Shunem epitomizes. Service conceived as "living among my own people," defined this Shunem *doulē*. She demonstrated a leadership that can be termed prophetic, in the sense that she maintained influence outside the sphere of the dominant power brokers, the king and the commander.

Unfortunately, the text, verses 12–13, that reveal the Shunammite's agency has remained unsung. These verses are excised from the readings in the Catholic Lectionary, which sets out the portions of the Bible assigned for reading in public worship.[9] The Catholic chosen and approved text read to the congregation silences the voices that highlights women's leadership role in this story. On the other hand, the text that highlights the woman as needy and helpless, someone in need of a son is included in the Lectionary reading. Expunging the liberative verses 12 and 13 that celebrate the female as subject represents another form of silencing. The selective reading of those sections of submission perpetuates women's invisibility. Evidently, the practice of omitting Scriptural texts that represent a positive female image denies not only women, but the people of God, the feminine face of God in the Scripture. Such denial deprives women of models of positive self-identification from the scriptural text. Justice both for women and for the people of God demands that the liberative verses in the narratives of the woman of Shunem need to be reinstated into the Catholic Lectionary. The metaphor of the *doulē* constitutes a channel through which to access and evaluate women's role. A redemptive reading of these texts could reconstitute, transform, and renew the community.

9. The Lectionary reading from this passage offered for Year A in Ordinary time has 2 Kings 4:8–11, 14–16.

We now turn to another piece of the mosaic, a contemporary *doulē* figure, Mother Mary Charles Magdalen Walker. Mother Walker understood the liberative effect of Scripture and appropriated same for service to the community way beyond her native homeland. Her prophetic role crystallized in her founding of an indigenous women's congregation, in Nigeria, the congregation of the Handmaids of the Holy Child Jesus.

MOTHER MARY CHARLES WALKER, RSC AND THE CONGREGATION OF THE HANDMAIDS OF THE HOLY CHILD JESUS

Mother Mary Charles Walker was English and belonged to the congregation of the Religious Sisters of Charity. Mother Mary Charles, empowered by an extraordinary gift of the Holy Spirit, offered herself for the mission in Southern Nigeria. Like a modern day Abigail, in 1923 Mother Mary Charles defied an impossible terrain to take up missionary activity in the vicariate of Southern Nigeria. Her determination to accept the ministry was not without controversy.

The objection from her superiors appeared to have confirmed and secured Mother Mary Charles' resolve. Irish historian and writer, Desmond Forristal noted that when the Sisters of Charity finally voted against Africa in 1921, Mother Mary Charles decided she would to go Nigeria on her own. Her fortitude stunned the community, their lawyers and the Archbishop of Dublin. Forristal captured their bewilderment thus, "The Sisters of Charity were aghast, the canon lawyers were aghast, the Archbishop of Dublin was most aghast of all.[10] It would be an understatement to suggest that the bewilderment of her superiors perhaps may have resulted from their inadequate comprehension of the power of the Spirit in the life of Mother Mary Charles. Because prophetic witness offers alternatives other than that which the establishment approves, such witnessing often must be co-opted or domesticated.

The providential, rather prophetic intervention of the Holy Father, Pope Pius XI, despite objections from local and ecclesiastical superiors, saved Mother Mary Charles' missionary vocation. The Pontiff responded in the affirmative to Mother Walker's petition to be part of the Nigerian Mission by issuing a rescript on 23 May 1923, granting her permission to

---

10. Forristal, *Second Burial of Bishop Shanahan*, 156.

join the Mission of Southern Nigeria. Writing for the Cardinal Bourne, Monsignor Surmount, the Vicar of the Westminster stated:

> By virtue of a rescript received from the Sacred Congregation for the Affairs of Religious in Rome and dated the 23rd of May, 1923, we hereby grant to Sr. M. Charles (Margaret Mary Walker) of the Institute of the Irish Sisters of Charity, 9 Chiswick Lane, London, permission to live out of her convent for the grave reasons known to her superiors.[11]

One can interpret the Pontiff's approval as a special form of missioning, in this case, by the universal Church The Pope's response met her hope that another world was possible for the thousands of children, women, and girls in need of guidance in the Vicariate of Southern Nigeria.

Fundamentally, Mother Mary Charles Walker's self-offering was to give Western education to girls and women and through this means share with them the Good News. She established convent schools and women's development centers as a means to achieve this aim. With such creative vision, she reimagined the women's role in colonial Nigeria. A brief family background would contextualize this modern day *doulē*, Mother Mary Charles Walker.

Margaret Mary Angela was born on 16 March 1881 to Edward Walker (an Army Colonel) and Josephine Woodhead, both of Brighton, England. The Walkers were solidly middle or upper middle class in Victorian England, noted for their consistency of academic performance.[12] The family converted to Catholicism from the Anglican Church before Margaret Mary Angela was born. The Walker girls, Margaret Mary and her two sisters, attended the prestigious Holy Child School at Mayfield, England. The school at Mayfield was "a very interesting school in which consummate skill in the art of teaching, unwearied patience, and the most persuasive personal influence have combined to accomplish all the rarest fruits of Christian instruction."[13] Young Margaret Mary Angela was shaped by this devoutly Christian milieu. The fifth of the Walker's six children, Margaret Mary Angela took the name Mary

---

11. Cooke, *Nun of Calabar*, 66.
12. Cooke, *Nun of Calabar*, 11.
13. Cooke, *Nun of Calabar*, 18.

Charles, at first profession of vows in the Congregation of the Religious Sisters of Charity (RSC), on 26 May 1904.[14]

The service of the Word, the Good News, constitutes the single motivating factor that brought Mother Mary Charles from England to Nigeria. Her passion to serve stands her in a prophetic stead. She stands alongside Israel's *doulas* and Mary of Nazareth, the *doulē kyriou,* in particular.

Mother Mary Charles' prophetic vocation was nowhere more evident than in her creative imagination, made manifest in her ability to foresee and respond to the situation in the mission in Southern Nigeria. Tested by criticism, suffering, and rejection, Mother Mary Charles, through patience and endurance, claimed this singular giftedness of prophetic leadership. She embodied her prophetic charism in a filial devotion to Mary, the *doulē kyriou,* by naming her new Foundation after Mary of the Annunciation, the Handmaids of the Holy Child Jesus (HHCJ).[15] Thus a prophetic call expressed in service and leadership legitimates the existence of this indigenous women's religious community from its origin. That is to say, the charism, which Mother Mary Charles embodied and handed down to the HHCJ, constitutes prophetic leadership in service. The new ecclesia community, the HHCJ, represents an alternative community for women, where they can grow and flourish following as their model the Lukan *doulē kyriou.*

Mother Mary Charles established the Convent school system for girls and young women. By this establishment, she rescued girls and young women from the role the dominant culture imposed, namely, uxorial duties. As an oasis for women in the early days of colonization in Nigeria, Mother Mary Charles' school confronted and confounded the dominant African men's thought of women.

Without doubt, most African men think of women as mothers, submerged in traditional families that impose on them women's and children's social circles dominated by male strategies. For these women, the village or rural community is their compulsory social and cultural reference point.[16] According to a "customary law" that the colonizers reshaped, an African woman remained a perpetual minor, a handmaid of a man, a *paidiskē,* one without social status, having neither voice nor

---

14. Cooke, *Nun of Calabar,* 12.

15. HHCJ, Constitutions, 6, 7.

16. Coquery-Vidrovitch, *African Women,* 233.

agency. The image of a woman as a handmaid of a man is very strong in many African societies. But research shows that these roles hardly agree with those of women in many traditional African societies. Holding on to a woman as a handmaid of a man has a negative impact on the continent as a whole. Women's subdued role in Africa robs the continent of the synergy of full human potential. In effect, any time a people exclude a large part of its population from full social participation, perennial poverty results. The inequalities among and within communities and nations, testify to the downside of power that excludes.

The schools became a system that stems the tide of poverty in the nation. The school provided an alternative to female domestication. Learning the art of reading and writing bridged the gender gap and placed women on equivalent footing with men. Education became like a new Pentecost. African women could become *doulas* in the sense of the Pentecost. It meant that women, just like men, could take up responsibilities as leaders in society and church life.

Obviously, women's education has not resolved the problems of imposed sexism. But the ability to read and write can truly become liberating when women can actually begin to represent their concerns. Women's solidarity can complement rationality to produce adequate emotional support that goes alongside a loving education. In such collaboration women's education can become truly liberative. This was the way Mother Mary Charles expanded and extended the potential of women within the Nigerian cultural context.

Over the centuries, the understanding of the Handmaid gathered patriarchal dust. Dust clouds vision and obscure possibilities. Caught in this situation, the HHCJ struggle with the renewal and re-envisioning of their founding charism, which is connected with the integral advancement of women, young girls, and children. Women were educated for their own soul-growth and not simply for the education of offspring. This singular approach enabled Mother Charles to raise from her pupils the foundation members of her new congregation: the Handmaids of the Holy Child Jesus (HHCJ). Her past pupils included women who later became prominent leaders in Nigerian civil society as well as mothers of many religious and priests, including Church prelates. The HHCJ, a community that represents what symbolizes an alternative for women continues to glean insights from the Annunciation narrative for inspiration to engage contemporary challenges.

The alternative community that the voices in the *Magnificat* proclaim, draws attention to witness to that which the Gospel constantly invites the women religious. The question becomes how the HHCJ and other African women religious can continue to sustain and maintain this alternative affinity to represent the authenticity of their call in the current epoch. How can the women religious read the Lukan passage from a contemporary prism in the quest for a hermeneutics that will join praxis and theology in the perspective of the Reign of God? The local community, is the arena where faith and practice come together. So an understanding of local traditions provides the warp in the weaving of a new cloth, the *akwete* imagery that form yet, another piece of mosaic that represents the new woman.

A WOMAN IN THE GLOBAL VILLAGE: RECLAIMING IDENTIFY

Bifurcation appropriately describes the world horizon of most Christians in the many African societies. Numerous factors contribute to the situation. Women's names, the subject of chapter four, is but an example. The divergent baptismal name produces a consciousness of its own. Some African theologians have identified this bifurcation as the root of the identity crisis in African Christianity.[17] But the hybridization of the two religious realities, African and "Christian" could necessitate the inclusion of plural views of the world culture. Such inclusion could become an effective tool of social change when properly understood and applied. Reclaiming tradition that valorizes personal names furthers the women's discourse.

That some female Igbo names sustain oppression has become obvious. A similar situation can also be attributed to the designation Handmaid, that which accompanies in a subordinate position, which can never be a subject, and always an object. The freight that a name carries can become a burden not only for the name bearer. By design, the effect on a single female so ill-named because of her sex extends to all females. Thus an under-determined appropriation of the name Handmaid can become problematic. Though battered, women could rebuild their image and seek healing and renewal caused by naming. Healing and rebuilding fits well into the image of the African-Igbo idea of *Mbari*.

---

17. Dedji, *Reconstruction and Renewal*, 3.

The representation of the *Mbari* depicts an elixir for a community struggling to redefine itself after devastation. *Mbari* constitutes a transitory shrine built to bring wholeness to the community after a major crisis. The most prominent figure in the *Mbari* represents "Mgbeke Nwaekpere." Mgbeke Nwaekpere is an exposed feminine image, a symbol of fertility, life and human flourishing. The construction of *Mbari* involves the entire community, evoking the "we-ethos," that sustains solidarity. In the *Mbari*, artists from the community depict the community's narrative individually and collectively through their artistic impressions. The idea of the *Mbari* shares family resemblance with Israel's building of the tent of meeting, the *ohel* or the tabernacle, a dwelling place of the divine presence in the community. As the children of Israel forged a sense of people-hood, everyone, men and women, contributed to erecting a befitting worship place that symbolized their sense of self (Exod 35:20–29). Unlike the Hebrew *Ohel* that was portable due to the wandering in the desert, the Igbo *Mbari* is sedentary. It is built where it is accessible to everyone in the local community. Each of the *Mbari* figures tells a story, a story of a particular aspect of the community and in some sense a story of the other figures independently, and jointly. Oduyoye summarized the *Mbari* motif thus, "Among the Igbo of Nigeria, to be creative is to turn the power of evil, sin and suffering into the power of love. When things are not going well in the community, in order to restore harmony and mutuality of existence, artists fashion a model of a whole community and all that they have in a house (*Mbari*), and the house and its artifacts are left as a sacrifice, which will renew the community."[18] These artists and storytellers, represent dreamers of an alternative history, a history that signifies the desired experience of the community. Retelling by recreating generates transgression, without which there can be neither discovery nor creativity. Creativity allows the differentiated aspect of women to flourish.

The healing and renewal that the *Mbari* figures evoke derives from the community's forceful identification with the symbols. Just as the *doulē* metaphor conjures up several images that represent healing and wholeness, women in contemporary Africa-Igbo society could deconstruct the female image sustained by the dominant culture by constructing their own version of *Mbari*.

---

18. Oduyoye, *Beads and Strands*, 14.

Evidently, the disruption of this particular tradition produced momentous changes in the traditional family life and society at large. Tradition used here refers to that body of lore and rules governing group boundaries and world-sense formation.[19] The American theologian Robert J. Schreiter contends that tradition, which serves as guarantor of resources for cohesion and continuity in a society, when disrupted causes a total breakdown of identity at either the individual or societal level.[20] Reclaiming gendered space, therefore, could provide the arena from which the plural views of bifurcated consciousness can become more intelligible. In this way, women can become again that symbol that renews the community in service and leadership secured in self-gift. In today's idiom, women could reconstitute the idea of gendered space to become a place where the female imaginative creativity can flourish again. From this seemingly bottom level of the social structures, but in truth, this capstone, women could begin to rebuild the social position that foreign influence disrupted.

The quest for human flourishing appears to reside in the realm of religion. This means that the ultimate destination of the process of identity-formation is located in the sphere of religion.[21] In addition, the significance of religion in social reconstruction represents that which the South African cleric and activist, Archbishop Desmond Tutu, discusses extensively in his book, *No Future without Forgiveness*. In this book, Tutu states clearly that religion plays defining roles in people's lives.[22] The Jewish people, for example, have continued to survive as a people because of their religious beliefs. Jewish particularism, namely, the practice of the Law, significantly influences Jewish consciousness. The Passover seder constitutes perhaps the greatest secret that has guaranteed Jewish identity, religious faith and tradition under difficult circumstances.[23] The power of religion in the extreme example of slavery demonstrates its potency. Schreiter's example of Christianity in South America and the Caribbean amplifies the idea of the fundamentality of religious traditions in the making and remaking of history. "In the Caribbean and in Brazil, elements of Catholicism were wedded to Ibo

19. Schreiter, *Constructing*, 106.
20. Schreiter, *Constructing*, 106.
21. Avis, *Eros and the Sacred*, 4.
22. Tutu, *No Future Without Forgiveness*, 81–82.
23. Spohn, *Go and Do Likewise*, 59.

and Yoruba religious systems of Africa to create new religious systems, which have by and large remained impervious to transformation."[24] The idea that religion represents a way of life for some people restates the grip that religion holds on a community. Proposing some elements in Scriptural traditions as agents for social change, therefore, compels hermeneutists to plumb religious traditions in a contextual reading of texts.

Undeniably, the import of religion on social construction can be constructive. It could provide an avenue for addressing women's issues from the very foundation of Igbo religious anthropology. Women's disadvantaged position, however, may result not from patriarchal structures, but from women's lack of knowledge of their heritage. This asks us to explore the link between memory and imagination.

Deprived of their narratives of origin, women can no longer dream dreams, nor have visions with which to reimagine the world they inhabit. Dreams and imagination represent the seed from which the future springs. Besides, the fact of possessing imagination means that everything can be redreamed, Okri posits.[25] When women begin to believe that each reality can have an alternative, then they can change the value they place on themselves and the world. Only at coming to this realization can women dare to redream their place in the world. Redreaming represents a beautiful act of imagination, and a sustained act of self-becoming—*doulē*, a servant as well as a leader. Without imaginative identification a person exists only as a distant spectator in ongoing history. Women could intentionally free themselves from the chains of culture and religion by taking up the challenges of biblical interpretation. Appropriation of the biblical religion foreground raises the theological possibility of seeing Christian women come into their own, into their rightful inheritance within their own cultural milieu. Only then can the "Redemption," the *Magnificat* be sung. Although Moses summoned the skills and learning he acquired, both in the court of the Pharaoh and as a shepherd, to confront the power of his day, the key to his success remained the cooperation of the people. Women's cooperation and solidarity represent perhaps the most viable option in achieving full participation in social processes. The notion of the *doulē* could truly act as a liberating metaphor, as well as a uniting vehicle for women. The

24. Schreiter, *Constructing*, 137.
25. Okri, *Way of Being Free*, 49.

idea of the *doulē* presents an attitude of wholesomeness. Its grounding in humility and service represents values cherished across religious traditions in Africa.

Conclusion

The *akwete* cloth captures the luminous image of a young woman who emerges from an obscure background to become a prophet in the hill country, because she understood herself as *doulē kyriou*. A critical reinterpretation of the *doulē* is crucial to women's advancement. Such reading could allow women to break away from the tutelage, which functional interpretation of the handmaid as *paidiskē* imposes. Like the Exodus, breaking away leads the community from servitude into service of the LORD. The effectiveness of the "break away" is secured in the formation of an alternative community that Mary sang in the *Magnificat*, a community that is covenanted with the God who promised to "be your God, you shall be my people" (Ezek 36:28).

The covenant is symbolized in Mary of Nazareth. By her *fiat*, she became a symbol of the sacred. She also represents the channel through which the *doulē* metaphor flows into the human heart and engenders human flourishing. The ideology of human flourishing expands the horizon to embrace other possibilities. This notion does not stand over and against reason like an object in the world. Rather the belief represents the goal of all human striving, a striving that enables people to dream dreams.[26] In this way, the *doulē kyriou* could become a potential representation of women's positive image and a paradigm of universality because service constitutes the very essence of the Christian life (Luke 22:27). In identifying positive strands in the old image of women and weaving them together with the new understanding of women, a sustained hope of self-becoming emerges, representing women's resplendence embodied in the gift of fostering the abundant life, *alafia, shalom, salaam, ndu na uju* (Yoruba, *Alafia*, Hebrew, *shalom*, Arabic, *salaam*, and Igbo, *ndu na uju* translates the term abundant life.) In so doing the *doulē* metaphor becomes a dignified condition in Africa because it aims preeminently at nurturing an adequate social transformation. The women discussed in this book were not lacking in initiative. They were not content with being "housewives" or a vegetative existence in the corner of the house

---

26. Kopfensteiner, "Globalization and the Autonomy of Moral Reasoning," 490.

of a man as the psalmist sings "Like a fruitful vine your wife within your home" (Psalm 128:3). There was not the case. These matriarchs were proactive. When thwarted by the male world or when they find it lacking in moral insight or practical initiative, they did not hesitate to take their destiny, or the nation's into their own hands. This, in effect, is the quintessential quality of the *doulē kyriou*, who can become a model of self-identification for women in society and church.

After more than three decades as a professed religious in community, the time has come for me to make a contribution toward rethinking women's situation in Africa and beyond. In rethinking, I have proposed a way forward for women, because the image of Mary in Christendom crosses the boundaries of cultures and Christian denominations. Muslims also identify with Mary, whom they designate Miriam, the mother of Jesus. Thus, the religious anthropology of Christians, and Muslims, provides us with female images with which to reconstruct women's identity in contemporary times. Employing none other than the image of Mary of Nazareth in the Lukan passage (Luke 1:2-38), underscores the importance of this project. The image of Mary can become the key that unlocks and makes possible a reinvention of the image of a woman. In assigning a key role to a woman at the beginning of his Gospel, Luke makes a case that God's reign will be socially transforming for those who dare to believe.

Glossary

Aku	Wealth
Daa	Honorific title for an older female
Dede	Honorific title for an older male
Ego	Money
Ihe	A thing
Ife, ihe	Brightness, luminosity, radiance, light, a thing, something.
Kwa	Again; an 'emphasis'; "too"
Mbari	"Decorated." *Mbari* is a transitory shrine built to bring wholeness to the community after a major crisis. Prominent figure in the *Mbari* represents "*Mgbeke Nwaekpere*," an exposed feminine image, a symbol of fertility and human flourishing.
Nmadu	A human person
Nkoli	Story; conversation.
Nnhe	A female species
Nwa	A child/offspring
Nwanyi	A female human person
Nwoko	A male human person.
Odibo	A servant, steward
Odozi	Keeper, steward, custodian
Ogu	War/fight
Ohù	A slave
Oke	Portion
Okhe	A male species
Uwa-t-uwa	"A World inside a world within a world, world without end"

Bibliography

Achebe, Chinua. "'Chi' in Igbo Cosmology." In *African Philosophy: An Anthology*. Edited by Emmanuel Chukwudi Eze, 67-72. Oxford: Blackwell Publishers, 1998.
———. *Anthills of the Savannah*. New York: Doubleday, 1989.
Adamo, David Tuesday. *Africa and Africans in the New Testament*. New York: University Press of America, 2006.
Agbasiere, Joseph Thérèse. *Women in Igbo Life and Thought*. London: Routledge, 2000.
Avis, Paul. *Eros and the Sacred*. Harrisburg, Pennsylvania: Morehouse Publishing, 1989.
Béchard, Dean P., ed. "Pontifical Biblical Commission, Document on the Interpretation of the Bible in the Church, September 21, 1993." In *The Scripture Documents: An Anthology of Official Catholic Teaching*. Collegeville, Minneapolis: The Liturgical Press, 2001.
Boss, Sarah Jane. *Empress and Handmaid: On Nature and Gender in the Cult of the Virgin Mary*. London: Cassel, 2000.
Bovon, Francois. *Luke 1: A Commentary on the Gospel of Luke 1:1-9:50*. Translated by Christine M. Thomas. Minneapolis: Fortress Press, 2002.
Brakke, David, Michael L. Satlow, and Steven Weitzman, eds. *Religion and the Self in Antiquity*. Bloomington, IN: Indiana University Press, 2005.
Brown, Raymond E. *An Introduction to the New Testament*. New York: Doubleday, 1996.
———. *The Birth of the Messiah: A Commentary on the Infancy Narratives in Matthew and Luke*. New York: Doubleday, 1993.
Brown, Raymond E., Karl P. Donfried, Joseph A. Fitzmyer, John Reumann. *Mary in the New Testament*. Philadelphia: Fortress Press, 1978.
Brueggemann, Walter. *The Word Militant: Preaching a Decentering Word*. Minneapolis: Fortress Press, 2007.
———. *The Prophetic Imagination*. Philadelphia: Fortress Press, 1981.
Buhner, J. A. "*Paidiskē*." In *Exegetical Dictionary of the New Testament*, volume 3, *pagideuw—wfelimos*, eds. Horst Balz and Gerhard Schneider. Grand Rapids, Michigan: Eerdmans, 1990.
Bujo, Bénézet. *African Theology in Its Social Context*. Translated by John O'Donohue. New York: Orbis Books, 1992.
Cooke, Colman. *Mary Charles Walker: The Nun of Calabar*. Dublin, Ireland: Four Courts, 1980.
Coquery-Vidrovitch, Catherine. *African Women: A Modern History*, Trans Beth Gillian Raps. Boulder, CO: Westview Press, 1997.
Davidson, Basil. *Africa in History*. London: Phoenix, 1991.
Dedji, Valentin. *Reconstruction & Renewal in African Christian Theology*. Nairobi, Kenya: Acton Publishers, 2003.

Diop, Cheikh Anta. *Civilization or Barbariam: An Authentic Anthropology.* Translated by Yaa-Lengi Meema Ngemi Editors Harold J. Salemson and Marjolijn de Jager. New York: Lawrence Hill Books, 1991.

Donahue, John R. "The Bible and Catholic Teaching: Will This Engagement Lead to Marriage?" In *Modern Catholic Social Teaching.* Edited by Kenneth R. Himes, 9–40. Washington, D.C.: Georgetown University Press, 2005.

Drury, John. "Luke." In *The Literary Guide to the Bible,* eds. Robert Alter and Frank Kermode, 418–39. Cambridge, Massachusetts: Harvard University Press, 1987,

Dube, W. Musa. *Postcolonial Feminist Interpretation of the Bible.* St. Louis, Missouri: Chalice Press, 2000.

Elwell, Walter A., ed. *Baker Encyclopedia of the Bible,* Volume 4. Grand Rapids, Michigan: Baker Books, 1997.

Fiorenza, Elisabeth Schüsler, ed. *The Power of Naming: A Concilium Reader in Feminist Liberation Theology.* New York: Orbis Books, 1996.

Fitzmyer, Joseph. *The Anchor Bible. The Gospel According to Luke (I—IX): Introduction, Translation, and Notes.* Garden City, New York: Doubleday, 1981–1985.

Forristal, Desmond. *Second Burial of Bishop Shanahan.* Dublin, Ireland: Veritas, 1990.

Frizzell, Lawrence E. "Worship, the Bond between Time/Space and Eternity: A Reflection on the Essays of Kenneth Schmitz and Matthew Lamb." *Nova et Vetera,* 4 no. 4 (Fall 2006): 851–56.

———. "Mary's Magnificat: Source and Themes." *Marian Studies,* Volume 50 (1999): 38–59.

———. "Mary and the Biblical Heritage." *Marian Studies,* Volume 46 (1995): 26–40.

Gabriel, Amakievi O. I. "The Dynamics of Culture and Feminism among the Izon and the Edo of the Niger Delta." In *Beyond the Marginal Land: Gender Perspective in African Writing.* Edited by Chioma Opara, 33–45. Port Harcourt, Nigeria: Belpot, 1999.

Gailey, Harry A. *The Road to Aba: A Study of British Administrative Policy in Eastern Nigeria.* New York: New York University Press, 1970.

Gebara, Ivone and María Clara Bingemer. "Mary." In *Systematic Theology: Perspectives from Liberation Theology.* Edited by Jon Sobrino and Ignacio Ellacuría, 165-177. New York: Orbis Books, 1996.

González, Justo L. *The Story of Christianity, Volume 2: The Reformation to the Present Day.* San Francisco: HarperSanFrancisco, 1985.

Green, Joel B. *The Gospel of Luke: The New International Commentary on the New Testament.* Grand Rapids, Michigan: Eerdmans, 1997.

Green, Margaret M. *Ibo Village Affairs.* New York: Frederick A. Praeger, 1964.

Richard M. Gula. *The Call to Holiness: Embracing a Fully Christian Life.* New York: Paulist, 2003.

Irvin, Dale T. and Scott W. Sunquist. *History of the World Christian Movement, Volume 1: Earliest Christianity to 1453.* New York: Orbis Books, 2005.

Iwuchukwu, Becky. "Women and Religion in Africa." In *Where God Reigns: Reflections on Women in God's World.* Edited by Elizabeth Amoah, 39–47. Accra, Ghana: Sam-Woode, 1997.

Hastings, Adrian. *The Church in Africa 1450–1950.* Oxford: Clarendon, 1996.

Johnson, Elizabeth A. *Truly Our Sister: A Theology of Mary in the Communion of Saints.* New York: Continuum, 2006.

Kalu, Ogbu U., ed. *African Christianity: An African Story*. Trenton, New Jersey: Africa World Press, 2007.

Kalu, Ogbu U. "Daughters of Ethiopia: Constructing a Feminist Discourse in Ebony Strokes." In *African Women, Religion, and Health: Essays in Honor of Mercy Amba Ewudziwa Oduyoye*. Edited by Isabel Apowo Phiri and Sarojini Nadar, 261–278. New York: Orbis Books, 2006.

Kopfensteiner, Thomas R. "Globalization and the Autonomy of Moral Reasoning: An Essay in Fundamental Moral Theology." *Theological Studies*, 54 (1993): 485-511.

LaVerdiere, Eugene. *Annunciation to Mary: A Story of Faith: Luke 1:26-28*. Chicago, IL: Liturgy Training Publications, 2004.

Leith-Ross, Sylvia. *African Women: A Study of the Ibo of Nigeria*. London: Routledge & Kegan Paul, 1965

Lozano-Vínz, Nora. "Ignored Virgin or Unaware Women." In *A Reader in Latina Feminist Theology Religion and Justice*. Edited by María Pilar Aquino, Daisy L. Machado, Jeanette Rodriguez, 204–16. Austin, Texas: University of Texas Press, 2002.

Maeckelberghe, Els. *Desperately Seeking Mary: A Feminist Appropriation of a Traditional Religious Symbol*. Kampen, The Netherlands: Pharos, 1994.

Magesa, Laurenti. *African Religion: The Moral Traditions of Abundant Life*. New York: Orbis Books, 1997.

Martin, Clarice J. "The Haustafeln (Household Codes)." In *Stony the Road We Trod: African American Biblical Interpretation*. Edited by Cain Hope Fielder, 206–31. Minneapolis: Fortress Press, 1991.

Mbiti, John S. *African Religions and Philosophy*, 2nd ed. London: Heinemann, 1990.

———. *An Introduction to African Religion*. London: Heinemann, 1975.

McLay, R. Timothy. *The Use of the Septuagint in New Testament Research*. Grand Rapids, Michigan: Eerdmans, 2003.

McManus, Jim. *All Generations Will Call Me Blessed: Mary at the Millennium*. New York: The Crossroad, 1999.

Meiselman, Moshe. *Jewish Woman in Jewish Law*. New York: Ktav Publishing House, 1978.

Menkiti, Ifeanyi A. "Person and Community in African Traditional Thought." In *African Philosophy: An Introduction*. Edited by Richard A. Wright, 157–68. Washington, D.C.: University Press of America, 1979.

Menn, Esther. "Prayer of the Queen: Esther's Religious Self in the Septuagint." In *Religion and the Self in Antiquity*. Edited by David Brakke, Michael L. Satlow, and Steven Weitzman, 70–90. Bloomington, Indiana: Indiana University Press, 2005.

Meyers, Carol. *Households and Holiness: The Religious Culture of Israelite Women*. Minneapolis: Fortress, 2005.

Meyers, Carol, ed. *Women in Scripture: A Dictionary of Named and Unnamed Women in the Hebrew Bible, The Apocryphal/Deuterocanonical Books, and the New Testament*. New York: Houghton Mifflin, 2000.

Muoneke, Romanus Okey. *Art, Rebellion and Redemption: A Reading of the Novels of Chinua Achebe*. New York: Peter Lang, 1994.

Gibellini, Rosino, ed. *Paths of African Theology*. New York: Orbis Books, 1994.

Newell, Stephen. "Devotion and Domesticity: The Reconfiguration of Gender in Popular Christian Pamphlets from Ghana and Nigeria." *Journal of Religion in Africa* 35, no. 3 (2005): 296–323.

Newsom, Carol A. and Sharon H. Ringe, eds. *Women's Bible Commentary*. Expanded Edition. Louisville, KY: Westminster John Knox Press, 1998.

Nussbaum, Martha and Jonathan Glover, eds. *Women, Culture and Development: A Study of Human Capabilities*. Oxford: Clarendon Press, 1995.

Nwabara, S. N. *Iboland: A Century of Contact with Britain 1860–1960*. Atlantic Highlands, NJ: Humanities Press, 1978.

Nwaigbo, Ferdinand. *Mary—Mother of the African Church: A Theological Inculturation of Mariology*. Frankfurt am Main: Peter Lang, 2001.

Nwokpo, Janet. *The Original Inspiration/Founding Charism of Mother Mary Charles Magdalen Walker, RSC (1881–1966)*. Enugu, Nigeria: SNAAP, 2002.

Nzegwu, Nkiru Uwechia. *Family Matters: Feminist Concepts in African Philosophy of Culture*. New York: State University of New York Press, 2006.

———. "Recovering Igbo Tradition." In *Women, Culture and Development: A Study of Human Capabilities*. Edited by Martha Nussbaum and Jonathan Glover, 444–65. Oxford: Clarendon, 1995.

Oden, Thomas C. *The Word of Life: Systematic Theology: Volume Two*. Second printing. Peabody, Massachusetts: Prince, 2001.

Oduyoye, Mercy Amba. *Introducing African Women's Theology*. Cleveland, Ohio: The Pilgrim, 2001.

———. *Daughters of Anowa: African Women & Patriarchy*. New York: Orbis Books, 1995.

Oduyoye, Mercy Amba and Musimbi, R.A. Kanyoro, eds. *The Will to Arise: Women, Tradition, and the Church in Africa*. New York: New Books, 2001.

Okeke-Ihejirika, Philomina E. *Negotiating Power & Privilege: Career Igbo Women in Contemporary Nigeria*. Athens, Ohio: Ohio University Press, 2004.

Okri, Ben. *A Way of Being Free*. Great Britain: Phoenix, 2002.

Okure, Mary Liguori. *A Profile of Mother Mary Charles Magdalen Walker, RSC (1881–1966) and her Daughters: The Handmaids of the Holy Child Jesus* (unpublished, 2008).

Okure, Teresa. "Hebrew: Sacrifice in African Perspective." In *Global Bible Commentary*. Edited by Daniel Patte, 535–38. Nashville, Tennessee: Abingdon Press, 2005.

———. "A New Testament Perspective on Evangelization and Human Promotion." *Journal of Inculturation Theology* 1, no. 2 (1994): 126–43.

Olajubu, Oyeronke. *Women in the Yoruba Religious Sphere*. Albany, New York: State University of New York Press, 2003.

Olupona, Jacob K., ed. *Beyond Primitivism: Indigenous Religious Traditions and Modernity*. New York: Routledge, 2004.

Olupona, Jacob K., ed. *African Traditional Religions in Contemporary Society*. St. Paul, Minneapolis: Paragon House, 1991.

Oyewumi, Oyeronke, ed. *African Gender Studies: A Reader*. New York: Palgrave Macmillan, 2005.

Pope Benedict XVI. "2007 World Day of Peace Message." *Origins* 36, no. 28 (Dec. 21, 2006): 439.

Ricoeur, Paul. *Interpretation Theory: Discourse and the Surplus of Meaning*. Fort Worth, TX: The Texas Christian University Press, 1976.

Rosenberg, Joel. "1 and 2 Samuel," in *The Literary Guide to the Bible*. Editors Robert Alter and Frank Kermode. Cambridge, MA: Harvard University Press, 1987.

Schneiders, Sandra M. *The Revelatory Text: Interpreting the New Testament as Sacred Scripture*. Collegeville, MN: Michael Glazier, 1999.

Schottroff, Luise, Silvia Schroer, and Marie-Therese Wacker. *Feminist Interpretation: The Bible in Women's Perspective*. Translated by Martin and Barbara Rumscheidt. Minneapolis: Fortress, 1998.

Schreiter, Robert J. *Constructing Local Theologies*. New York: Orbis Books, 2003.

Seim, Turid K. *The Double Message: Patterns of Gender in Luke-Acts*. Nashville, Tennessee: Abingdon Press, 1994.

Siker, Judy Yates. "Blessed One: Protestant Perspective on Mary." *Review of Biblical Literature*, 6 (2004): 559–62.

———. "Unmasking the Enemy: Deconstructing the 'Other' in the Gospel of Matthew." *Perspective in Religious Studies*, 32 no. 2 (Summer 2005): 109–23.

Smallwood, E. Mary. *The Jews under Roman Rule: From Pompey to Diocletian, A Study in Political Relations*. Boston: Brill Academic Publishers, 2001.

Spohn, William C. *Go and Do Likewise, Jesus and Ethics*. New York: Continuum, 2000.

———. *What Are They Saying About Scripture and Ethics?* New York: Paulist Press, 1995.

Sugirtharajah, R. S. ed. *Vernacular Hermeneutics*. Sheffield, England: Sheffield Academic Press, 1999.

Sugirtharajah, R. S. *Postcolonial Reconfigurations: An Alternative Way of Reading the Bible and Doing Theology*. St. Louis, Missouri: Chalice Press, 2003.

Tarr, Del. *Double Image: Biblical Insights from African Parables*. New York: Paulist, 1994.

Tepedino, Ana Maria and Margarida L. Ribeiro Brandao. "Women and the Theology of Liberation." In *Mysterium Liberationis: Fundamental Concepts of Liberation Theology*. Edited by Ignacio Ellacuría and Jon Sobrino, 221–31. New York: Orbis Books, 1993.

The Constitutions of the Handmaids of the Holy Child Jesus. *Behold the Handmaid of the Lord*, 1985. Approved by D. Simon Cardinal Lourdusamy, Head of the Office of the Propagation of the Faith in the Vatican.

Tolbert, Mary Ann. "Defining the Problem: The Biblical and Feminist Hermeneutics." *Semeia* 28, no. 1 (1983): 132–26.

Turner, Victor. *Image and Pilgrimage in Christian Culture*. New York: Columbia University Press 1978.

Ukpong, Justin S. "New Testament Hermeneutics in Africa: Challenges and Possibilities." *Neotestamentica* 35, no. 1-2 (2001): 147–67.

Uzukwu, Elochukwu E. *A Listening Church: Autonomy and Communion in African Churches*. New York: Orbis Books, 1996.

Van den Heever, Gerhard. "On How to be or Not to be: Theoretical Reflection on Religion and Identity in Africa." *Religion and Theology* 8, no. 1 (2001): 1–25.

Walker, Alice. *In Search of Our Mothers Gardens: Womanist Prose*. Orlando, Florida: Harcourt Brace, 2003.

Watt, Harrington David. "The Meaning and End of Fundamentalism." *Religious Studies Review* 33, no. 4 (October, 2007): 269–73.

West Gerald O. and Musa W. Dube, eds. *The Bible in Africa: Transactions, Trajectories and Trends*. Leiden: Brill. 2001.

Wilder, Amos. *Theopoetic Theology and the Religious Imagination*. Philadelphia: Fortress Press, 1976.

Wimbush, Vincent L. "Signifying on Scriptures." In *Feminist New Testament: Global and Future Perspectives*. Edited by Kathleen O'Brien Wicker, Althea Spencer Miller, and M. Musa W. Dube, 245–58. New York: Palgrave Macmillan, 2005.

Wright, Benjamin G. "'Ebed/Doulos': Terms and Social Status in the Meeting of Hebrew Biblical and Hellenistic Roman Culture." *Semeia*, no 83–84 (1998): 83–111.

———. "*Doulos* and *Pais* as Translations of 'BD: Lexical Equivalences and Conceptual Transformation." In *IX Congress of the International Organization for Septuagint and Cognate Studies*, 263–77. Atlanta, GA: Scholar, 1997.

Yezierska, Anzia. *Bread Givers: A Struggle between a Father of the Old World and a Daughter of the New*. New York: Persea Books, 1975.

www.ingramcontent.com/pod-product-compliance
Lightning Source LLC
Chambersburg PA
CBHW060915190426
43197CB00012BA/2512